# Educational Technology
## Leadership Perspectives

# EDUCATIONAL
# TECHNOLOGY
# LEADERSHIP
# PERSPECTIVES

**Greg Kearsley & William Lynch**
The George Washington University
**EDITORS**

**EDUCATIONAL TECHNOLOGY PUBLICATIONS**
**ENGLEWOOD CLIFFS, NEW JERSEY 07632**

**Library of Congress Cataloging-in-Publication Data**

Kearsley, Greg, 1951–
    Educational technology:  leadership perspectives / Greg Kearsley &
William Lynch.
       p.  cm.
    Includes bibliographical references (p.   ) and index.
    ISBN 0-87778-265-2
    1. Educational technology--United States.    2. Educational
leadership--United States.    I. Lynch, William, 1952–
II. Title.
LB1028.3.K43  1994
371.3'078--dc20                               93-11504
                                            CIP

Printed in the United States of America.

Library of Congress Catalog Card Number:
93-11504.

International Standard Book Number:
0-87778-265-2.

*First Printing: January, 1994.*

# Preface

There are many books and courses about leadership in education. However, anyone aware of the pervasive problems in our school system would wonder if any of this information about leadership ever gets applied. Most of these problems can be attributed to poor leadership skills—an area in which many teachers and administrators admit they need improvement and more training.

This book addresses the topic of leadership in the use of educational technology. Over the past decade, technology has come to play an increasingly prominent role in schools around the world. More and more teachers and administrators use technology in some aspect of their daily activities. There is a tremendous need for leadership in the use of technology to ensure that it makes a valuable and lasting contribution to education.

We hope that this book will provide a useful introduction to the nature of educational technology leadership. It consists of three sections: Issues, Examples, and Strategies. The chapters in the first section discuss some of the issues associated with leadership in the use of educational technology. In the second section, a number of case studies of leadership are presented that range from technology in single schools to efforts of a national scale. The third section includes chapters that outline various strategies for leadership in the domain of educational technology.

It is important to realize that there are many different views of leadership and many successful ways to lead. Each of the chapters in this book embodies a somewhat different perspective on what constitutes leadership in the domain of educational technology. However, there are also many common elements to these different perspectives. For example, the concept of "vision" and a focus on well-defined goals are central to most discussions of leadership. Similarly, communication and persuasion skills are critical abilities of any leader.

A few words about the contributors are in order. In addition to being well-known experts in the field of educational technology, they are also all leaders. This book provides an opportunity for them to describe their views of leadership, sometimes in quite personal terms. Even though most of the contributors now reside at universities or research organizations, it is important to realize that almost all have extensive experience in schools and industry. Indeed, the chapters contain much practical wisdom and "lessons learned."

By presenting a variety of different perspectives of leadership in educational technology, we hope that this book will stimulate discussion about the relative success of alternative approaches. We also hope that it will stimulate more educators to adopt leadership roles with respect to educational technology. Historically, educational leadership has been largely left to chance. We believe this is a serious mistake; all educators should have opportunities for the critical analysis and practice of leadership.

All royalties from this book go to the Mentor Endowment Fund of the ECT Foundation established by the Association for Educational Communications and Technology (AECT). We hope this will help to provide scholarships and financial assistance to students who wish to pursue their studies in the field of educational technology leadership.

Greg Kearsley
William Lynch

# Foreword

As a magazine and book publisher serving the field of educational technology since 1961, I bring a different point of view to this volume than that held by the authors of the following chapters. My role has been that of an observer and leader-as-idea-disseminator, rather than as a genuine *doer* in the field. I stand in awe of those individuals, represented by the authors of the chapters in this book I am pleased to publish, for they have been out in the field day by day actually doing what people such as myself can only talk about achieving. And they have been initiators of new ideas—indeed new paradigms or ways of thinking about educational reality—in an area of human endeavor that is renowned for its tradition-mindedness—some would even say its hide-bound, die-hard resistance to change.

I have witnessed the evolution of educational technology through many waves of bold new ideas, techniques, and media followed by counter-waves of reactions and interactions. Among these have been teaching machines and programmed learning, instructional systems design, computer-based training, performance technology, interactive video and multimedia, educational systems design, and on and on.

Each of these movements and sub-movements has had its own set of adherents (and, always, opponents). Some have arisen out of earlier ideologies and/or technologies, while others have come apparently out of the environment of our times, with no particular educational background, just ideas "waiting to happen" and sparked by numerous non-educational events and happenings in the larger society.

Within this torrent of ideas, we have seen different kinds of leadership, in a continuum in which one becomes more and more effective and influential. What I find most interesting about this spectrum of leadership in the field of educational technology is that in just about all cases it is necessary, in fact essential, for each individual to progress through all of the stages. It is only the very rare person who moves immediately to the broadest possible leadership mode—it simply does not happen with ordinary individuals, that is, virtually all of us.

First, with regard to technology in education, we find that one becomes enamored of a single technology as explicated in the form of a piece or a system of hardware. In the early 1960s this was the Teaching Machine. In the late 1970s and early 1980s this artifact or medium was the microcomputer. Today it's "interactive multimedia."

Next, it is discovered that hardware, while necessary, is hardly sufficient. Indeed, it begins to dawn on some people—the new leaders—that the hardware is not nearly as important as the *software* that is mediated by the machine.

The third stage of leadership emerges as people begin to see that the technology, in the form of hardware and software, can only be truly effective if it integrated into the total fabric of the educational environment, rather than remaining as enclave or system in itself.

Finally, we came to the stage of leadership in which individuals began to see that what *really counts* is the ability to envision the total design of learning environments. The technology of hardware-software systems then becomes part of the larger technology of the systematic and systemic design and redesign of teaching and learning.

Many educators never make the leap from hardware to software to integration to total systems design. Fortunately, we need the talents of those who are concerned not with large systems but with the (relatively) simple tasks of how to design effective computer software. We need people who wish to undertake the tasks of integrating computers and other technologies into schools and other centers of learning and human development.

We see the full range of leadership efforts in this volume, moving from teacher-leaders, concerned with how to use computers to improve their own teaching efforts, to those designing entirely new systems of education.

It is my hope that we continue to encourage and honor educators at all stages of the leadership spectrum. Yet, it seems to me that all leaders benefit considerably from trying to take the widest possible point of view. It is when one sees educational technology in its full context that he or she can be *most* effective. How does computer-based training fit into overall efforts to improve our schools? Where, when, how do we best use interactive multimedia instruction? Can distance learning via telecommunications be utilized as a lever to change educational outcomes? Any of these technologies, employed in a vacuum, can be effective, at least within a limited scope. Clearly, though, when each is viewed holistically as part of a larger framework of educational technology—as building blocks for a systematic and systemic design of learning—the sum becomes much more than an accumulation of its parts.

I am pleased to see this first of what I hope will be many volumes on aspects of educational technology leadership. We need visionary leadership here, as we do elsewhere in our complex world, as we approach the turn of the new millennium.

Lawrence Lipsitz
Publisher

# Contents

# Educational Technology
## Leadership Perspectives

# Part I: Issues

This first section includes four chapters that focus on the underlying issues in educational technology leadership and raise fundamental questions about the subject to be addressed throughout the book.

In Chapter 1, Kearsley and Lynch examine the nature of leadership and argue that leadership in the domain of educational technology is different in certain respects from educational leadership in general. This includes a thorough understanding of what particular technologies can (and can't) accomplish, the technology planning process, and factors that affect implementation success. It is also argued that there are many different levels of leadership needed in educational technology and different kinds of skills associated with each level. The chapter ends by discussing the nature of training programs needed to prepare educators to carry out leadership roles in educational technology.

In Chapter 2, Dede discusses four critical components of leadership in educational technology: (1) envisioning opportunities where technology could make a contribution, (2) displacing cherished notions, (3) inspiring others to act on faith, and (4) discouraging "followers." The last component (which gives rise to the chapter title) is a measure of successful leadership according to Dede because it means that the innovation has been accepted widely enough to be sustained beyond a single champion.

Almost all contributors to this volume agree on the essential nature of "vision" to successful leadership. In Chapter 3, Rhodes discusses how such a vision must be articulated and shared with the entire learning community affected by technology. Rhodes describes the nature of the envisioning process underlying the Christa McAuliffe Institute. She also outlines the most important aspects of change that are brought about by innovations. One of her major arguments is that everyone affected by technology must understand the nature of change and this is one of the primary tasks of leadership.

While we usually think of technology in terms of its instructional applications, it also plays a pivotal role in school administration and management. In this context, administrators demonstrate leadership through the use of technology to improve the efficiency and effectiveness of school functions. In Chapter 4, Bozeman and Spuck discuss the evolution of administrative computing and the increasingly wider range of applications that technology can impact. They emphasize the potential of technology to improve the decision-making skills of school administrators, and hence their leadership abilities.

# 1/ Educational Leadership in the Age of Technology: The New Skills[1]

## Greg Kearsley & William Lynch

**The George Washington University**

*This chapter analyzes the concept of educational technology leadership. It is argued that leadership in the domain of educational technology is different in various ways from leadership in general. In particular, the skills underlying technology leadership need to be identified so they can be incorporated into training programs for teachers and school administrators. The chapter concludes that understanding such skills is a critical research area because many educational technology efforts fail due to lack of good leadership at all levels of school systems.*

Instructional technology has come to play a major role in the U.S. educational system. Computers are widely used in the nation's schools. Industry and the military makes extensive use of teleconferencing, interactive video, and simulators. Instructional design techniques and theory are commonly employed in the development of major curriculum projects and training materials. Systematic planning procedures and evaluation methods are used in most large school districts and training organizations.

However, the results of technology use in the classroom have been equivocal. Analysis of the effectiveness of technology in education (e.g., Cuban, 1986; OTA, 1988; Saettler, 1990) suggests that the manner in which technology is implemented is more important than any intrinsic characteristics. In other words,

---

[1]An earlier version of this chapter appeared in the *Journal of Research on Computing in Education*, Volume 25 (1).

leadership of one kind or another plays a very critical role in the success of instructional technology.

While Schools of Education and school systems have made progress in their efforts to train teachers in the use of instructional technology (e.g., Glenn & Carrier, 1989), there has been little critical examination of technology leadership, i.e., the factors that are associated with the exemplary use of technology in schools. Outstanding technology educators are publicly recognized (e.g., *Educational Technology* Magazine's Person of the Year in Educational Technology, the *Electronic Learning* Computer Educator of the Year Award, the *Computer Learning Foundation* Outstanding Lesson Plans, the Christa McAuliffe Educators) but the factors that underlie their success are not clearly articulated. It will be difficult to properly prepare teachers or administrators to assume leadership roles with instructional technology until there is a better understanding of technology leadership.

It is important to understand the historical context of this issue. Most teachers had little opportunity to use and learn about advanced technology until the early to mid-1980s when computers and video technologies became affordable and widely available. This means that the majority of teachers have less than a decade of experience using technology in the classroom. These teachers are just now reaching the senior teaching and administrative positions in our school system where they will have significant influence on educational practice and policies. For this reason, it is critical to start studying the issue of technology leadership now so that the current and future cohorts of school leaders can be prepared to deal more effectively with technology.

This chapter provides a conceptual framework for the analysis of technology leadership. Of particular interest is the identification of skills that make up such leadership qualities so they can be incorporated into suitable learning activities for teacher training programs. We begin with a short discussion about the nature of leadership in education.

## Leadership Research

An understanding of technology leadership shares much with research on leadership in general, and educational leadership in particular. It is our contention, however, that the specific knowledge and abilities involved in technology leadership deserve special attention. Technology leadership is inherently linked to innovation and this provides unique considerations. While leadership usually involves dealing with change, technology leadership deals almost exclusively with new procedures, policies, and situations. A critical element in technology leadership is the ability to develop and articulate a vision of how technology could produce changes (Cory, 1990).

There are many conceptualizations of leadership ranging from the classic trait theories to behavioral and contingency theories (e.g., Burns, 1978; Tannenbaum,

Wechsler & Massarik, 1961). While all of these different theories contribute to our understanding of leadership, we believe that a cultural view of leadership is most useful in the domain of education and technology leadership. The cultural view of leadership (e.g., Schein, 1985; Sergiovanni & Corbally, 1984) suggests that the success of leaders is determined by their ability to articulate and influence cultural norms and values. Leaders are expected to shape the culture of individual schools and school systems by creating new visions which organizational members can believe in and act upon. More recent work has focused on the concepts of empowerment and shared leadership at all levels (e.g., Maxcy, 1991; Sergiovanni, 1990).

Technology of one form or another has always been part of the formal educational system in the form of books, chalkboards, duplicating machines, teaching systems, and managerial strategies. The use of mechanical and electronic technologies, however, have typically been looked upon as radical departures from a humanistic vision of teaching and learning (e.g., Oettinger & Marks, 1969; Turkle, 1984). Generally, teachers have also lacked training or experience with these types of technology, leaving them in an insecure and unskilled position with respect to their use in the classroom. Additionally, the experiences provided with poorly planned or supported innovation attempts have often left teachers floundering—with a mandate to use technology but without a strong sense of how, why, or to what end.

Many reasons can be cited for the relative failure of mechanical and electronic technologies in education including a lack of good training and appropriate materials, poorly conceived implementation plans, unrealistic goals or expectations, and insufficient funding. Most of these problems, however, can be corrected with time, attention, and appropriate actions. A fundamental lack of belief in the innovation, however, will ultimately prove to be the death of even the best conceived plan. Users of technology need to be converted to a point of view; they need to believe that what they are being asked to do will work and that it is the best available solution to an identifiable educational problem. Users should also be bound by a political allegiance to a technological solution; they should be willing to support the allocation and reallocation of resources for solutions they believe in. Finally, users need to know that they will have the technical expertise and support required to maintain the technology in a form consistent with the technology's appropriate use.

Leaders engage in building shared values and beliefs and then attempt to sustain the cultural system with social and technical support structures. A technology leader, however, must be specifically skilled in conceiving technical solutions to identified educational problems and then building theoretical, political, and financial support structures to ensure the success of the solution. Any kind of strategic behavioral change, if it is to be successful as a long-term solution, must be supported by prior affective changes in the participants. In other words, everyone involved in the change process, from top to bottom, must believe in what they are doing or the inertia generated by innovation for its own sake will quickly disappear. Without the prerequisite culture building and concomitant support, technological solutions will predictably deteriorate into superfluous pedagogical bandages or boondoogles.

Such culture building may result in new administrative procedures, teaching methods, personnel policies, and curriculum. Change can occur at the school level or throughout the school system, and each calls for different levels of leadership. At each level, there are specific skills that must be acquired in order to be a successful technology leader.

## Levels of Skills

In order to address the  specific leadership skills required for technology, it is important to focus on the different levels/roles involved. Table 1 lists some examples of skills needed at five levels: State, District, Principal, Teacher, and Technology Specialist. This Table and discussion is based upon Collis (1988).

Table 1 presents a listing of managerial requirements for technology leaders at a variety of organizational levels.  It is argued that all of these skills are essential to educational technology leadership. What is not listed in each category are those general qualities that need to be present at all levels.  For example, culture building or a commitment to a set of beliefs and values must occur at each level. While the specific values will vary from the state level to the individual school or classroom, the process of creating shared beliefs will be very similar. Emotional and political support for technology innovation also needs to exist at each level.  Technology leaders must know what population to work with and, then, through a combination of managerial skills, personal communication, and influence, "lead" the way to a visionary reality.

One important point to observe about these levels is that leaders do not have to be administrators. In fact, much instructional technology leadership comes from teachers who have informally accepted responsibility for encouraging and supporting other teachers, students, and staff in their use of technology. There are advantages and disadvantages to this kind of "grassroots" or bottom-up type of leadership. The main advantage is that such leadership is driven by genuine convictions and first-hand experience. The main disadvantage is that this kind of leadership can be very idiosyncratic and limited by the parochial interests of the particular individuals involved.

Another significant point is that leadership does not come only from individuals.  Committees, development groups, support groups, subject-centered teams, and associations may all play leadership roles. In fact, it is very important that leadership functions not be stratified. Although there are some functions which must be handled administratively at certain organizational levels, leadership for these functions can be shared by individuals and groups from all

Table 1
Examples of Technology Leadership Skills
(Adapted from Collis, 1988.)

### I. State Level
• establish a common format for data processing across districts
• negotiate discounts for district hardware and software purchases
• support regional technology centers
• set standards for teacher training in technology
• maintain a state-wide educational computer network
• conduct evaluations of technology in schools
• specify policies for copyright enforcement

### II. District Level
• identify specific objectives for technology use in schools
• coordinate hardware/software purchasing and maintenance
• ensure integration and communication among all levels of schools
  with respect to technology use
• plan and conduct teacher and staff inservice training
• coordinate district-wide administrative computer use
• provide special services and equipment relevant to district needs

### III. Principals
• ensure equal access and opportunity to technology resources
• establish policies for ethical use of technology
• ensure facilities for technology are appropriate
• establish priorities for technology use in school
• provide released time for technology training
• reward outstanding technology applications
• seek out funding sources for technology

### IV. Teachers
• use teaching techniques that fully exploit technology
• encourage parental involvement with technology
• match technology applications to needs of students
• look for cross-curriculum/cross-cultural applications
• facilitate cooperative student applications
• use technology to improve personal efficiency

### V. Technology Specialists
• provide personal support to teachers/staff
• develop new applications of technology
• identify educational problems for which particular technologies
  may provide solutions
• articulate technology problems and promise across all administrative levels
• disseminate information about technology
• encourage ethical behavior (e.g., copyright)
• introduce new software or hardware
• recommend/evaluate software or hardware
• troubleshoot software/hardware problems

organizational levels and, at the least, input should be solicited from all these levels before any final decision is made. This process is, of course, cumbersome, but effective when permanent and long-term change is desired. This realization that leadership must be distributed across the full educational constituency is a critical aspect of current school restructuring efforts in the U.S. (e.g., Pearlman, 1989).

The five levels outlined in Table 1 are proposed in the context of the U.S. educational system. However, it is suggested that a similar multi-level hierarchy of leadership skills will be necessary in any country. One of the interesting questions about this conceptual framework is the extent to which it applies to developing nations which are just beginning to embrace educational technology in their school systems.

## Consequences of Leadership

What are the benefits and problems associated with good and poor technology leadership? The potential benefits of good technology leadership can include:

- improved academic achievement by students;
- improved student attendance and reduced attrition;
- better vocational preparation of students;
- more efficient administrative operations; and
- reduced teacher/staff burnout and turnover.

Over the years, it has been amply demonstrated that in certain learning situations, the use of technology can improve student achievement relative to current methods (e.g., Bosco, 1986; Kulik, Bangert & Williams, 1983; Niemiec & Walberg, 1987; Roblyer, 1988). More importantly, the use of technology can present students with more meaningful and interesting learning activities. This outcome explains why technology can influence student attendance and attrition—if students find school more challenging and relevant, they come more often and stay longer. The use of technology in the classroom puts them more in synchrony with the needs of most employers. For example, when students learn to use word processing or spreadsheet software in their classes, they are better prepared to enter the workforce, not necessarily because of the specific skills that they possess, but because of the sense of potential productivity that such skills represent.

There are many ways that technology can improve the administrative operations of a school system or individual school (Bluhm, 1987; Kearsley, 1990). Examples include optical test scoring systems that speed up grading; student registration and class scheduling systems that minimize the effort required in these tasks; word processing and desktop publishing systems that reduce the time and costs of producing letters, reports, and proposals; and highly specialized software for monitoring building heating, managing food preparation, or generating optimal bus routes.

The last benefit mentioned on the list above, reducing teacher/staff burnout and turnover, is often overlooked but vitally important. Many teachers and staff members report that the use of technology introduces a new challenge to their jobs (Kearsley, Hunter & Furlong, 1992). Coupled with some of the benefits already mentioned, this challenge renews their interest and enthusiasm for teaching or administration. There is, however, a potentially negative side-effect of this benefit; teachers and staff members who become very proficient with technology become externally valued and are often lured out of the education system into private industry.

Some of the common problems associated with technology use in education (e.g., Becker, 1987; Dwyer, Ringstaff & Sandholtz, 1990; Sheingold & Hadley, 1990) can be attributed to poor technology leadership, including:

- lack of knowledge about how to use technology (resulting in ineffectual usage);
- lack of adequate time or funds to properly implement technology;
- use of technology for its own sake rather than genuine need;
- unequal access creating "have" and "have-not" groups;
- poorly designed facilities resulting in limited access;
- poor results resulting in negative attitudes about technology; and
- overt resistance on the part of potential users.

Lack of knowledge about how to use technology is very common at all levels of education. Failure to provide adequate training (either enough or the right kind) is the usual reason underlying this problem. The amount of time required to learn how to use a new program (whether it is a teacher learning how to use an instructional program or an administrative assistant learning how to use a purchasing system) is often underestimated. Furthermore, most people require "hands-on" practice to properly learn a system; such practice is often overlooked or too minimal.

Related to this problem is the lack of adequate time or funds to implement technology, usually due to inexperience and poor planning. Successful implementation of technology almost always takes more time and money than initially expected. For example, when implementing a local area network in a school building, modifications needed for the cabling or incompatibilities with existing software may be overlooked. When acquiring computer equipment, the additional costs of security, insurance, or air conditioning may not be foreseen.

One of the more insidious problems is the adoption of technology for its own sake. Responding to public, school board, or vendor pressures, administrators will often go along with the implementation of a particular technology even though it does not respond to any real school need. Teachers, staff, and students must then struggle with a technology that has no value to them. This problem is especially acute with "technophiles" who are not happy unless they have the latest technology.

Unless care is exercised, the problem of unequal access can easily arise. Technology may be appropriated by certain groups for their own use and not be shared across all subjects or with all students. For example, computers may be acquired by the mathematics department for use with gifted and talented students—thereby shutting off this resource to the rest of the school. Alternatively, a lab and equipment may be set up for remedial learning with "at risk" students—again with the same results. Certain schools may be technology-rich, while others lack any, or lack up-to-date equipment.

The fundamental point of this discussion is that possession of the kinds of leadership skills described in the preceding section are essential to ensure that the potential benefits of technology are realized and that the possible problems are avoided. General leadership skills are necessary but not sufficient when it comes to technology; specific technology-related knowledge is required. In the next section, we turn to the question of how and where these skills are to be acquired.

## Leadership Training

The preceding discussion has a number of implications for the training of technology leaders. There are three principal entities where such training occurs: Schools of Education, state and local educational agencies, and professional organizations. Ideally, these three entities can work in a coordinated manner to provide comprehensive technology leadership training.

The training of teachers about technology is routine by Schools of Education and state/local educational agencies. Almost every college and university in the U.S. that trains teachers offers at least one instructional technology course (e.g., Ely, 1988). Similarly, most large school districts run regular inservice workshops on technology. However, these courses tend to focus on operational skills, i.e., how to use technology to teach, rather than the conceptual and strategic issues involved in technology leadership. Teachers who complete a graduate degree in instructional technology may go into these issues on their own but not in any systematic manner. Thus, even the teachers who become technology specialists in the school system may not have had any formal training in technology leadership.

One area that is especially important for technology leadership is the ability to critically evaluate existing and new technology. For example, there are many social and philosophical implications of technology in schools (e.g., Bowers, 1988; Lynch, 1990) that are not addressed in the usual technology courses. We need educators who can think about the possible side-effects and human impact of technology and weigh these consequences in their decision-making. We do not want a generation of "technocrats" any more than we want "technophobes."

It is interesting to consider the technology leadership question from the perspective of what teachers who use technology say they need. A study by Wiske *et al.* (1988) that involved a national sample of such teachers reports the following needs: (1) easy access and availability of suitable hardware and software; (2) guidance in how to use computers effectively in their classrooms; (3) adequate training and follow-up assistance; (4) layers of support including aides, computer coordinators, colleagues, and sympathetic principals; (5) more influence on technology policy; and (6) more research on effective strategies of computer use. These needs suggest areas that training in technology leadership should address.

One of the critical areas of technology leadership training that has been largely ignored is school administrators. Few administrators at any level have received formal preparation for instructional technology. In general, they have learned what they do know about technology through informal experiences and observation. In many cases, administrators depend completely on teachers or technology specialists (and, in a few cases, vendors) for guidance.

It is possible to give administrators a reasonable grounding in the fundamental concepts and issues during a single semester university course (Kearsley, 1988), yet most Schools of Education do not offer such courses for school administrators. One organization that stands out in this respect is the Institute for the Transfer of Technology to Education (ITTE) of the National School Boards Association. The ITTE is focused on how to make schools more productive through the use of technology. The ITTE Technology Leadership Network helps administrators at hundreds of schools interact on a regular basis through meetings, site visits, and conferences.

## Conclusions

It is our conclusion that teachers and administrators are not being properly prepared to promote and manage technology in schools. This conclusion is based upon the many cases where technology is inappropriately or ineffectually used and by the almost complete absence of any specific training focused on technology leadership. There is a critical need to establish formal training programs for teachers and school administrators in technology leadership. The outline of such a program is shown in Table 2.

The objectives of such a program are intended to match the skills outlined in Table 1. Educational technology leaders need to be able to use technology to solve real problems in schools. In order to do this they must understand the strengths and limitations of various technologies as well as the conceptual issues underlying any application of instructional technology. They must know how to

Table 2
Technology Leadership Training Program

*Goal:*
To develop individuals capable of improving our educational system through the wise use of instructional technology.

*Objectives:*
• Conceptualize and design technology-based solutions to educational problems.
• Know and employ strategies that result in the successful implementation of technology-based educational solutions.
• Explain and predict the changes that adopting a new technology will entail.
• Understand the strengths and limitations of current and emerging technologies.
• Conduct evaluations of technology including formative and cost/benefit studies.
• Understand the conceptual and theoretical issues underlying the application of instructional technology.

*Topics:*
• Computer Applications in Teaching and Learning
• Computer Applications in Educational Administration
• Educational Hardware Systems
• Organizational Dynamics
• Leadership Theory
• Instructional Theory & Design
• Program Evaluation
• Educational Policy Studies
• Instructional Software Design
• Distance Education
• Interactive Multimedia
• Educational Systems Design

successfully implement technology and be familiar with the type of changes that adoption of technology will entail. They must also be able to conduct and interpret evaluations of technology in terms of cost-benefits and educational impact.

In order to address these objectives, a wide selection of topics need to be covered. This includes current and emerging applications of computers in teaching and administration. It also includes theory and practice in leadership, policy studies, and program evaluation. At some levels of leadership (e.g., technology coordinator), it will be necessary to go into the details of educational hardware, instructional software design, interactive multimedia, and distance education. A case study approach is high desirable to sensitize students to the many variables involved and how they interact (e.g., Blomeyer & Martin, 1991).

Programs such as this should be offered as graduate level study at Colleges of Education and as professional workshops by school districts and professional organizations. In most cases, this type of program would be taken by individuals who already had some background and experience with technology. It is our belief that teachers and administrators who take these programs will exhibit the kind of technology leadership skills that will ultimately lead to much more effective use of technology in our educational systems.

## References

Becker, H. J. (1987, July). *The Impact of Computer Use on Children's Learning: What It Has Shown and What It Has Not.* Baltimore, MD: Johns Hopkins University.

Blomeyer, R. & Martin, D. (1991). *Case Studies in Computer Aided Learning.* Bristol, PA: Falmer Press.

Bluhm, H. (1987). *Administrative Uses of Computers in Schools.* Englewood Cliffs, NJ: Prentice-Hall.

Bosco, J. (1986, May). An analysis of evaluations of interactive video. *Educational Technology, 26(5),* 7–17.

Bowers, C. A. (1988). *The Cultural Dimensions of Educational Computing: Understanding the Non-Neutrality of Technology.* New York: Teachers College Press.

Burns, J. M. (1978). *Leadership.* New York: Harper & Row.

Collis, B. (1988). *Computers, Curriculum, and Whole Class Instruction.* Belmont, CA: Wadsworth Publishing Co.

Cory, S. (1990). Can your district become an instructional technology leader? *The School Administrator (Special Issue on Technology),* 17–19.

Cuban, L. (1986). *Teachers and Machines: The Classroom Use of Technology Since 1920.* New York: Teachers College Press.

Dwyer, D., Ringstaff, C. & Sandholtz, J. (1990, April). The evolution of teachers' instructional beliefs and practices in high access to technology classrooms. *AERA Conference Proceedings,* Boston, MA.

Ely, D. (1988). Trends and issues in educational technology. In B. Branyan-Broadbent & R. K. Wood (Eds.), *Educational Media & Technology Yearbook*. Englewood, CO: Libraries Unlimited.

Glenn, A. D. & Carrier, C. A. (1989). A perspective on teacher technology training. *Educational Technology, 29(3)*, 7–12.

Kearsley, G. (1988, November). What should today's school administrators know about computers? *THE Journal, 16,* 34–38.

Kearsley, G. (1990). *Computers for Educational Administrators: Leadership in the Information Age*. Norwood, NJ: Ablex.

Kearsley, G., Hunter, B. & Furlong, M. (1992). *We Teach with Technology*. Wilsonville, OR: Franklin, Beedle & Associates.

Kulik, J. A., Bangert, R. L. & Williams, G. W. (1983). Effects of computer-based teaching on secondary students. *Journal of Educational Psychology, 75(1)*, 19–26.

Lynch, W. (1990). Social aspects of human-computer interaction. *Educational Technology, 30(4)*, 26–30.

Maxcy, S. J. (1991). *Educational Leadership*. Westport, CT: Greenwood Publishing Co.

Niemiec, R. & Walberg, H. J. (1987). Comparative effects of computer-based instruction: A synthesis of reviews. *Journal of Educational Computing Research, 3(1)*, 19–37.

Oettinger, A. & Marks, S. (1969). *Run, Computer, Run*. Cambridge, MA: Harvard University Press.

Office of Technology Assessment, U. S. Congress. (1988). *Power On! New Tools for Teaching and Learning*. Washington, DC: Government Printing Office.

Pearlman, R. (1989, June). Technology's role in restructuring schools. *Electronic Learning*, 8–56.

Roblyer, M. D. (1988, Sept). The effectiveness of microcomputers in education. *THE Journal*, 88–95.

Saettler, P. (1990). *The Evolution of American Educational Technology*. Littleton, CO: Libraries Unlimited.

Schein, E. H. (1985). *Organizational Culture and Leadership*. San Francisco: Jossey-Bass.

Sheingold, K. & Hadley, M. (1990). *Accomplished Teachers: Integrating Computers into Classroom Practice.* Center for Technology in Education, Bank Street College of Education, New York.

Sergiovanni, T. J. (1990). *Value-Added Leadership.* San Diego, CA: Harcourt Brace Jovanovich.

Sergiovanni, T. J. & Corbally, J. E. (1984). *Leadership and Organizational Culture.* Chicago: University of Chicago Press.

Tannenbaum, R., Wechsler, I. & Massarik, F. (1961). *Leadership and Organization: A Behavioral Science Approach.* New York: McGraw-Hill.

Turkle, S. (1984). *The Second Self.* New York: Simon & Shuster.

Wiske, M. S., Zodhiates, P., Wilson, B., Gordon, M., Harvey, W., Krensky, L., Lord, B., Watt, M. & Williams, K. (1988, March). *How Technology Affects Teaching.* Educational Technology Center, Harvard Graduate School of Education, Cambridge, MA.

## About the Authors

*Greg Kearsley* is an Adjunct Professor of Educational Leadership at the George Washington University in Washington, DC. Dr. Kearsley has written numerous books and articles in the field of educational technology. He received his Ph.D. from the University of Alberta in 1978.

*William Lynch* is an Associate Professor of Educational Leadership and Director of the Educational Technology Leadership program at the George Washington University in Washington, DC. Dr. Lynch received his Ph.D. from the University of Maryland in 1984.

# 2/ Leadership Without Followers

## Christopher J. Dede

**George Mason University**

*What are the qualities of leadership in educational technology? In this chapter, Dede discusses four critical components based upon personal experience: (1) envisioning opportunities, (2) displacing cherished misconceptions, (3) inspiring others to act on faith, and (4) discouraging "followers."*

The concept of leadership is fraught with misconceptions. People often see leadership as a combination of meticulous management, adept political maneuvering, and responsive facilitation of others' activities. While each of these is important in advancing the field of educational technology, I believe the true nature of leadership is exemplified by the four attributes below.

## Leadership Requires Envisioning Opportunities

One of the most important attributes that distinguishes leaders from managers is "vision": the ability to communicate desirable, achievable futures quite different from where the present is drifting. Leaders create and convey compelling images of how our reach is much less than our potential grasp; they redefine people's paradigms about what is possible. In contrast, competent managers are adept at organizing operations so that an institution's efficiency in accomplishing plans is optimized. This is a vital task often neglected by leaders who do not understand management, to their later regret, for good administration involves both envisioning and operationalizing.

At present, educational technology offers many opportunities for leadership because every aspect of its context is rapidly shifting. The information technologies are evolving very quickly: merging, adding powerful capabilities, decreasing in cost. The global economy is changing the skills American workers

*19*

must have, emphasizing both technical excellence and intercultural design for the worldwide market. Simultaneously, the U.S. population is becoming more diverse, pluralistic: a salad bowl rather than a melting pot. Society's conception of the educational system's role is also in flux; at the heart of current movements for reform and restructuring is a desire to move beyond fine-tuning present models to redefining the nature of schooling.

Over the next decade, all these external forces will combine to drive major shifts in the mission, curriculum, clients, and process of educational institutions (Dede, 1992a). Whether these changes actually improve learner outcomes will depend in large part on the quality of the visions we forge during the 1990s. The challenges we confront require a new, better paradigm for schooling; the power of emerging technologies enables implementing models for teaching/learning unique in the history of civilization. The noted American philosopher, Yogi Berra, is said to have stated that if you don't know where you are going you are likely to end up someplace else. The opportunities for leaders in educational technology to invent innovative visions are boundless.

Developing motivating images that capture the essence of needed changes is important, but insufficient to make educational technology a driveshaft for reform. Leadership also involves creating stepping stones that bridge from a desired future to the current gridlock typical of many American schools. In evolving from its present state to a distant objective, an educational institution must progress stage by stage. Each step of evolution requires a critical mass of resources and must create a stable, desirable situation.

When I share ideas, I present trends and discontinuities that are driving major changes in our societal context and can serve as the basis for stepping stones to the future. Some of these developments have a negative impact in the short-term, but long-term open up possibilities for educational evolution. For example, society's immediate response to economic crises is to cut back on instructional innovations, but in the long run financial hardship can drive needed changes by forcing schools to abandon ineffective approaches that have hardened into traditions.

Other developments, such as advances in educational technology, create new possibilities for improving teaching/learning. As one illustration, digital video technology allows the synthesis of computer graphics and video images, enabling the television generation to see and manipulate visual representations of abstract, intangible concepts (Dede, 1992b). Developing visions that transcend how emerging capabilities enhance conventional schooling to depict their implications for empowering new paradigms is vital. Ultimately, digital video is not simply a more powerful tool for teachers' presentations, but also enables inexpensive multimedia authoring by students. By constructing their own knowledge structures, learners gain a much deeper understanding than by simply assimilating a pre-packaged multimedia experience.

In my talks and articles, I describe how we can act today to take advantage of these technological innovations, building on their impacts to actualize new models for schooling. I also emphasize how political, economic, demographic, and sociocultural forces will affect this process of attempted transformation, empowering some changes while repressing others. A credible, desirable vision is based on both opportunities and challenges. Without levers for improvement, significant gains in educational effectiveness are unlikely; without troubles, society will not shift from drifting through the present to implement alternative paradigms for teaching/learning.

My presentations give a balanced picture of where we are in history—both the good news and the bad news—to demonstrate that a hopeful image of the future can emerge from turbulent, uncertain, even dangerous times. Synthesizing optimistic/pessimistic perspectives on technical, political, and economic themes into a compelling future image is very demanding; one must be an intellectual omnivore with an emotional stance midway between hope and cynicism. I have found cultivating this professional outlook to be challenging; slipping into optimism or pessimism, becoming a technophile or a "doubting Thomas" are constant, subtle traps. However, maintaining a balanced perspective conveys the reward of visions that are detailed, plausible roadmaps to desirable futures.

How does one develop and maintain this discipline of dispassionate, integrative envisioning? I have found the following heuristics useful:

- Seek out sources of information that you find intellectually stimulating, especially if you instinctively disagree with their conclusions. Informed, but opposing points-of-view enrich visions.
- To broaden your ideas, find sources of information good at explaining material outside of your professional area (e.g., if you don't understand artificial intelligence, read authors who synthesize/translate recent work for a lay audience).
- Reflect on the quality of recent events in your personal/professional life (things going well? badly?) and compensate for that emotional bias in your images of the future.
- Keep an open mind about revising your prior visions as the world changes. Getting stuck in a particular flavor of futures is a seductive pitfall.

Above all, remember that the leader's goal in envisioning the future is not to construct intriguing speculations, but to incite transformative action in the present.

## Leadership Requires Displacing Cherished Misconceptions

An important attribute of leaders is their ability to displace deeply held, cherished misconceptions with alternative visions that more accurately depict reality. Mistaken beliefs most people hold about teaching and learning form a barrier that blocks improving American education. For example, many in our culture have a subconscious image of the secondary school that is based on the following assumptions:

- despite coming from diverse cultural and socioeconomic backgrounds and going through puberty, just below the surface teenagers have a strong work ethic and a fascination with intellectual pursuits;
- regularly attending PTA meetings and sports events, paying taxes, and electing dedicated school board members provides sufficient parental support for quality education;
- because they are deeply fulfilled by their impact on learners' lives, highly qualified teachers will enter and stay in the profession despite low salaries, marginal working conditions, and little respect from the community;
- schools should be settings isolated from the real world in which learners are grouped by age and taught the academic disciplines as formal subjects;
- students are graduating into a future workplace in which mastery of the skills that multiple-choice tests can measure will guarantee them a fulfilling, prosperous career; and
- technology's utility in education lies in automating routine activities that underlie this model of schooling and in motivating learners via instructional formats analogous to video games and television.

Unfortunately, all these assumptions that underlie this image of the secondary school are fundamentally inaccurate (Dede, 1990a). As a result, intensively applying technology to improve this model of education (e.g., integrated-learning systems and computer labs, multimedia-based teacher presentations, more elaborate testing) results in only small improvements in outcomes.

Shifting communities to alternative visions for education that are based on more realistic, but less comfortable assumptions is a major leadership challenge. In abandoning the old model of secondary education, parents and businesses and teachers and students must confront some unpleasant truths about our culture's current weaknesses. For schools to succeed, parents must provide time and effort as well as money; an excellent teaching staff may cost more than most communities are willing to pay; many students do not have middle-class values and aspirations; and the skills for future occupational success in the global economy are quite different from what can be conveyed by test-oriented, subject-centered group instruction in classrooms remote from real-world settings.

Leadership requires packaging alternative assumptions and paradigms as part of a larger vision that inspires new roles for educational stakeholders. In my work, I use scenarios as a means of undercutting "conventional wisdom" by highlighting potential futures quite different from present models of schooling. Here is one example (Dede, 1990a):

> Dr. Hari Grosvenor sat on the floor with his students in a circle. Three 6-year-olds were trying to talk simultaneously. Each was somewhat impeded in the discussion by having to use Spanish (this part of the day was devoted to practice in a second language), but their enthusiasm was unhindered. To Hari's relief, only his handicapped student's instructional device was currently in the room; he hated information technology.
>
> Hari felt that intelligent tools had their uses, but not in his classes. The foundations for his pupils' discussion had been laid by technologies that trained them in the prerequisite knowledge, but only a human teacher could master the intricacies of teaching a seminar. His specialty was helping learners with low self-esteem feel capable, loved, motivated, and challenged. Hari reveled in the freedom he had: to teach anything he wanted in any way he chose, so long as his students' sense of personal worth increased. His ability to assess individual learning style better than the most sophisticated diagnostic devices was being studied, but he knew that a machine could never replace him.
>
> From her vantage point at the far side of the circle, safely in the middle of her pressure pad, Ariel watched Hari deftly refocus the discussion. The scanner on top of her computer screen continually monitored Ariel's actions with her wooden blocks. Simultaneously, icons on the screen depicted her movements, text along the screen's bottom described her actions, and a synthesized voice in her earphones discussed what she was doing. Her congenital mental handicap was rapidly improving through this immersion in multiple representations of reality, from concrete manipulations to abstract symbols plus the care of her teachers. Still, she liked her machine best of all right now; no person was as oblivious to her handicaps.
>
> Having intervened to stop his seminar from coming to blows over who should serve as their representative on the school's governing board, Hari's thoughts wandered. He wondered how he should spend his merit bonus; once again, his innovation quotient had been the highest in the school. "Computers slow down those other teachers and stifle their creativity," he mused. "I'm glad the next stage in the master plan for our region calls for less reliance on instructional devices. Biotech prosthetic enhancers are definitely the best thing going."

Hari's merit bonus for innovation, his freedom to control content and methods as a way of building learners' self-concept, and the participation of students in school governance exemplify assumption-breaking innovations essential for successful restructuring. Ariel's sophisticated technological aids, which serve as an external nervous system, provide a provocative contrast with Hari's "anti-technological" stance.

Incorporating humor into these vignettes provides a framework for discussing the obsolescence of current approaches in a motivating, rather than discouraging manner. These scenarios also depict new roles educational stakeholders might play without bogging down in the immediate mechanics of how to bridge to these futures from the present; the intent is to provide a sketch rather than a blueprint. In counterpoint to assumption-breaking scenarios, however, television's "situation-comedy" classrooms convey opposite images that reinforce cherished myths in our culture. Undercutting society's mistaken beliefs about teaching/learning requires both attacking these myths and advancing compelling alternative ideas.

Since our society frequently uses gadgets as magical remedies in attempting to solve social problems, moving beyond the conventional wisdom of educational technology as "silver-bullet" is difficult. In our field, leadership requires developing both instruction-oriented technologies and technology-intensive learning-by-doing approaches; applying this combination of pedagogical strategies necessitates numerous assumption-breaking changes in the organizational context of the classroom and the roles of teachers, parents, and students. Creating and conveying technological visions powerful enough to displace traditional educational models is one of the most challenging aspects of leadership.

How does one identify obsolete paradigms and forge visions that encourage alternative conceptions? An excellent resource on the intellectual processes underlying scenario building is Peter Schwartz's *The Art of the Long View* (1991). The following strategies have been particularly helpful for me:

- Start with the central change you wish to foster, then identify all the major factors (inside and outside the organization) shaping that issue. This process highlights the driving forces to include in alternative visions and frequently surfaces underlying, conventional assumptions to question.
- Rank key assumptions and driving trends on both their importance to the change you wish to create and the degree of uncertainty surrounding their continuation. The most important and uncertain factors form the basis for differentiating alternative scenarios.
- Build each vignette around some type of story: how a particular group responds to a major challenge to their way of life, how the evolution of a technology reshapes an organization, how the assumptions underlying a traditional approach erode and are displaced by new ideas. The intent

is to provide a "snapshot" of some future time, hinting at the "movie" that could provide a path from our present to that vision.

- Make sure that the scenario is constructive in presenting the change process: depicting the advantages for every group involved; positive about people's willingness to adapt; portraying the challenges to be overcome in a realistic, but humorous manner. Invoking an attainable image involves constructing a vision that all major stakeholders find desirable.

The creative formulation of assumption-breaking visions can be one of the most enjoyable aspects of leadership; breaking the invisible chains that bind our minds is very stimulating.

## Leadership Requires Inspiring Others to Act on Faith

Inspiring a group to work toward a shared vision necessitates building trust: faith that this team of people can overcome all the obstacles that block creating a future quite different from the present. We often speak of visions as "dreams" because we do not believe they are possible; we doubt that they can be made real. Actualizing a plan for the future involves harnessing people's emotions as well as their minds, developing both understanding and belief.

The psychological stability of the present impedes our ability to emotionally invest in a future divergent from established trends and traditions (Dede, 1990b). We know that earthquakes or assassinations, winning the lottery, or scoring a sensational come-from-behind victory are statistically inevitable, but we are surprised when they happen because the commonplace nature of most events undercuts our belief in discontinuities. When someone can prove that a desired future is logical, rational, and inevitable, then any competent manager can persuade an institution to act. The challenge of leadership is to inspire individual and organizational faith in the seemingly impossible, developing a collective affective commitment that can move mountains of impediments.

By evolving so rapidly that each new development seems almost magical, information technology provides a fertile medium for nurturing trust that educational transformation is achievable. The availability and affordability of tools powerful enough to reshape learners and schools can help create the emotional motivation to risk innovation. Leaders build on the enthusiasm that sophisticated technologies induce to encourage an affective climate that rewards risk-taking and accepts occasional failures as an inevitable byproduct of developing new approaches.

Building shared trust in a vision requires a type of emotional charisma that goes beyond having good ideas. By accomplishing apparently unachievable outcomes themselves, leaders instill confidence in their collaborators. By never wavering in commitment and in certainty that the goal will be reached, leaders inspire similar faith in others. Would-be innovators who rely solely on intellectual suasion reap applause, but not action.

This dimension of leadership keeps me humble about the impact I have through making speeches. While an inspiring talk can have considerable emotional impact by sowing motivating ideas about information technology's role in education, it is only the first step in achieving sustainable change. I view my writings and conference presentations as good catalysts for innovation; because these activities reach a wide audience, they are among the most important things I do. I also recognize that the possibilities of lasting improvement are remote unless local leaders use my visions as part of an infrastructure to provide both intellectual and emotional support for reform. On the other hand, as an outsider to the local group, I can discuss unpleasant truths and build credibility for challenging policies (the "visiting fireman" syndrome— an expert is always someone from more than fifty miles away).

Shooting a few silver bullets and riding out of town is a seductive role, but comprehending the limited nature of the outcomes this behavior produces is important. Leaders understand that their success depends on combining the wisdom of the sage with the emotional nurturance of the healer or minister. Building faith and trust is essential in converting a group's understanding to shared, sustained accomplishment. This is particularly true with educational technology, since many hours of effort are required to realize the potential of sophisticated hardware and software. Despite the "plug and play" protestations of the vendors, developing technology-intensive educational strategies requires substantial emotional commitment and frequent leaps of faith into the unknown.

How does one inspire an organizational environment of shared risktaking and trust? *The Fifth Discipline* by Peter Senge (1990) is a good resource for ideas; recipes for success are hard to give, because so much depends on your particular interpersonal style. Approaches I have learned include:

- Make the process of change personally rewarding to participants: people like to learn new skills, to be part of a team, to feel successful by overcoming a challenge, to find the humor in shared adversity. Focusing on process enables the change effort to keep going even if a particular strategy fails; if outcomes are seen as the only measure of success, a group's first setback will destroy its effectiveness.
- Help others to see that their personal identity extends beyond their current job. We live in a culture that places too much emphasis on individual work roles as a source of self-worth. Refocusing emotional perspective on new missions within the purpose of the overarching enterprise (empowering society's next generation of human resources, rather than being a seventh grade social studies teacher) opens up new reservoirs of motivation and purpose.

Two final thoughts on this aspect of leadership: First, if everyone in your organization likes you, you are not fostering enough change. Second, if you never fail, you are not taking enough risks.

## Leadership Requires Discouraging "Followers"

A destructive myth about leadership is that a visionary person gives directions to followers who execute this plan. Real leaders discourage followers, instead encouraging use of their visions as a foundation for other, better insights. True solutions to problems are always based on ideas from multiple perspectives; no individual, however capable, can incorporate the full range of knowledge and experience needed to invent an educational system that fulfills the needs of a diverse community.

When leaders who surround themselves with followers fall from grace or move on, the innovations they have inspired collapse or wither. Sustainable transformations require stakeholders who fully understand the what and how of the vision and who act together (top-down, middle-out, bottom-up) to evolve dreams into realities. Technologists have often erred in setting themselves up as wizards who understand the magic in the black box. Instead, a leader in educational technology should inculcate others' visions, knowledge, and commitment to the point that all are jointly leading. This requires moving beyond the role of team facilitator or coordinator, acting as an exemplar by deliberately following others instead of always leading.

Emotionally, shedding the power and rewards of authority is very difficult. We all secretly long to be the superstar in front of the worshipping audience, to inspire awe and reverence. Like any other social movement, educational technology has generated some leaders who degenerated into gurus. Worse, many potential leaders have abdicated their responsibilities to instead assume the comfortable mantle of discipleship, blindly following someone else's vision. Condemning leaders seduced by power is easy and fun; recognizing the times each of us has avoided the difficult path of leadership to become a follower is hard and painful. Educational reform can achieve genuine, lasting success only when each stakeholder accepts the responsibility of leading.

In conclusion, leadership is a role fraught with difficulties, requiring both wisdom and maturity. Yet my goal in articulating the requirements of leadership is to encourage everyone to lead, always. If each of us were to act in the ways described above every day, however imperfectly, educational technology could be the driveshaft for restructuring education and shaping a bright future for our society.

# References

Dede, C. (1990a). Imaging technology's role in restructuring for learning. In K. Sheingold & M. S. Tucker (Eds.), *Restructuring for Learning with Technology*. New York: Center for Technology in Education, Bank Street College of Education, and National Center on Education and the Economy.

Dede, C. (1990b). Futures research and strategic planning in teacher education. In R. Houston (Ed.), *Handbook of Research on Teacher Education*. New York: Macmillan.

Dede, C. (1992a). Education in the 21st Century. *Annals of the American Association for Political and Social Science, 522,* 104–115.

Dede, C. (1992b). The future of multimedia: Bridging to virtual worlds. *Educational Technology, 32(5),* 54–60.

Senge, P. (1990). *The Fifth Discipline: The Art and Practice of the Learning Organization*. New York: Doubleday.

Schwartz, P. (1991). *The Art of the Long View: Planning for the Future in an Uncertain World*. New York: Doubleday.

## About the Author

*Christopher J. Dede* is a Professor at George Mason University in Fairfax, Virginia, where he has a joint appointment in the Schools of Information Technology & Engineering and of Education. He directs the Center for Interactive Educational Technology and is on the faculty of GMU's Institute for Public Policy. His research interests span technology forecasting and assessment, artificial intelligence, data visualization, and strategic planning. He received his Ed.D from the University of Massachusetts.

# 3/ Sharing the Vision: Creating and Communicating Common Goals, and Understanding the Nature of Change in Education

## Donna C. Rhodes

**National Foundation for the Improvement of Education**

> *Before any kind of fundamental changes can be made in a school or district, a "vision" for students must be created, understood and shared by teachers, administrators, parents and the entire "learning community." This chapter discusses creating and communicating a vision, and understanding the nature of educational change.*

Situated in between the oil fields and rolling hills of McKittrick, California, is the Belridge School—the only school in the Belridge School District. The Belridge School District has what every district in the country dreams of: an abundance of tax revenues to be used to improve the education it provides for its students. In 1988, the Belridge District decided to create a "community of global learners."

Further up the Pacific coast in Washington state is the Central Kitsap School District. Several years ago, this district, home of numerous schools serving over 11,000 students, also decided to improve the education its students received. However, unlike the Belridge School District, Central Kitsap had limited tax revenues to invest in improvements. Despite their differences, both districts adopted ambitious plans to restructure their schools.

Belridge officials bought every student and teacher two computers—one for school and one for home. The school acquired extensive video equipment, laser discs, and a television station. Students were sent home early one day a week so teachers could attend training classes on using the new technologies as teaching tools. Curriculums were redesigned to include collaborative projects that stimulated critical thinking and problem-solving. In sum, the school's talented teaching force and supportive principal adopted many of the elements needed to improve education and prepare students for the 21st Century.

But the project at Belridge fizzled after only two years. In contrast, Central Kitsap, with many more students and stretched resources, now serves as a national model of successful change in education. In 1988, the Kitsap District introduced "Strategy 2020," a plan designed by teachers, administrators, parents, and other community members to "lay a foundation for lifelong learning." The plan proposed many of the same changes in curriculum and uses for technology as Belridge, but had to make certain adjustments for less equipment and larger classes.

Why, under seemingly ideal circumstances, did Belridge's efforts not go as planned, while Kitsap, with its more challenging situation, succeed?

At Kitsap, the entire community participated in creating a vision of education for its students. At Belridge, only the teachers and administrators were involved in designing the project and identifying the results they wanted to achieve.

Lasting change in education of any scale or scope—from changing a science curriculum to charting a new assessment system—can succeed only if everyone touched by the change understands and shares the same vision of how the change will work to improve education for students. Teachers, administrators, parents, and the entire "learning community" must be involved in envisioning and planning change from the very beginning.

In many ways, the first step that must be taken if a project aimed at bringing about educational improvement is to succeed is the most difficult. Before any plan is put in place, all those who have a stake in the outcome of the project— teachers, administrators, parents, other community members, and when possible, students—must be able to identify what they want to occur. This sounds elementary, but many decision-makers conclude change is necessary, without first determining exactly what the change should ultimately mean for students. In other words, they don't identify the "student-outcomes" that are the goals of working to make their visions real. Student-outcomes must be the driving force that shapes all decisions made about change, and each change should move the learning community one step further toward its vision of improved education.

In Central Kitsap, Strategy 2020 was developed by teachers, administrators, parents, and other community members. They realized their first task was to determine the kind of learning environment they wanted to create and the skills they wanted their students to have. After much reflection and discussion, they agreed they wanted their students "to become active learners, equipped with the knowledge, attitudes, and skills essential for them to be happy and successful and contribute to a rapidly changing and diverse society." In this one sentence, they articulated their vision of what they wanted to achieve. Subsequently, all decisions made about the kinds of changes that would take place in Kitsap—changes in instruction, curriculum, and teaching tools including technology—were designed to further this vision.

## Scenario-building

Visions of improved education become more focused through a process called "scenario-building." Scenario-building is describing, in detail, a snapshot picture of what a vision made real will mean to a particular group. In education, scenarios might describe a student's or teacher's day in the envisioned school of the future. Scenarios breathe life into theories and ideas, and the process of creating scenarios helps those involved in planning change have a better understanding of how to proceed.

Scenario-building was the first stage of the National Foundation for the Improvement of Education's Learning Tomorrow program, a program dedicated to helping educators further their restructuring efforts by using technology. NFIE brought together teachers, administrators, futurists, parents, and experts in the field of technology to describe scenarios of what rural, urban, and suburban schools of the future might be like for students. Following is an excerpt from one scenario developed for Diana, a 21st century student attending an urban or suburban high school.* Note how such a description illustrates how changes in curriculum, instruction, and teaching tools work to further an overall vision of student learning:

> Diana's day begins with "introspection." This is time set aside for the students to meditate and reflect on past, current, or future activities—and clear the mind.
>
> Diana then starts the "knowledge" portion of her day. She attends an integrated subject class, where multiple subjects are taught based on a theme. This week, the students discovered several artifacts in the research fields located on the school grounds. They established an archaeological dig site, and have uncovered several peculiar objects that have given them clues about a civilization that existed there many years ago.
>
> Diana's social sciences class is studying about these past civilizations and cultures. They are using telecommunications to search data bases on the topic and locate information about the artifacts they discovered. Diana sends a message through the laptop computer's modem at her student workstation to a student in foreign language class. She asks him to help translate a script found scrawled on one of the objects. Next, Diana decides to participate in an archaeological field trip in Cancun—she is able to do this by using an interactive videodisc player. She travels through the ruins, choosing many

---

* Taken from the NFIE publication, *Images of Potential*.

different paths. Along the way, she collects in-depth information on digging techniques.

Diana's math class is working on designing a three-dimensional computer graphic simulation of the dig site. The students are working closely with the science class to determine the appropriate dating techniques to ascertain the age of the artifacts.

[The scenario goes on to describe Diana's newspaper reports on the dig for her English class, a special "Thinking Skills" class she attends, and other activities.]

It's clear that the authors of the scenario had a "vision" for Diana and her peers. This vision included the following: students learning to work in collaborative groups, completing meaningful projects incorporating different academic subjects, acquiring and honing higher order thinking skills, and using technology as a tool for learning.

Scenario-building helps everyone involved in envisioning and working toward the creation of successful learning environments understand how specific changes might affect students, teachers, schools, and the community in the years to come. Scenarios are a powerful tool for communicating a vision clearly.

When developing scenarios, it's important *not* to place limitations on what's envisioned. Money for new technology, time for teacher-training, plans for organizing community support, and all the activities necessary for achieving a vision should be considered later. Communities must concentrate on creating a learning environment that will achieve the goals set for students, no matter how different the scenario is from their present situation.

When NFIE began planning its Christa McAuliffe Institute—a program that was to honor teachers for their pioneering efforts and encourage them to be "risk-takers"—concerns about money and time constraints dictated the original design. When the plan was presented to NFIE's Board of Directors, it was labeled pedestrian and boring. So NFIE staff went back to the drawing board, and pushed limiting thoughts aside. The staff designed its ideal program, opting to overcome budget restrictions and other restraints as they occurred. Today, the McAuliffe Institute is an exciting, innovative program that encourages pioneering educators to expand their efforts and help others do the same. It validates teacher risk-taking—something that the program itself had to do before it could be successful.

The risks teachers in the McAuliffe program take are in bringing their own visions to fruition. To help the teachers facilitate this process, the Institute involves them in another kind of scenario-building—not just about new kinds of learning and learning environments, but about how change can take place in their schools.

Each year, the McAuliffe Institute selects a theme and honors five teachers who are pursuing innovative work related to that theme. These teachers are named Christa McAuliffe Educators. The Institute then solicits proposals from teams of teachers who have designed projects related to the theme. Teams with the most promising proposals are named Christa McAuliffe Fellows and are invited to join the Educators for a two-week summer conference at Stanford University. During the conference, the entire group explores the theme in great detail, and the Fellows refine their project plans. The group also creates scenarios about how change might take place in their schools, and discusses how new ideas are implemented. The scenario-building exercises prepare them for the time when they'll return to their schools and begin to translate their visions into practice.

For example, when the Institute announced its 1989 theme, "Preparing All Students for the 21st Century: Teaching with Technology for Diversity and Change," Myrna Peterson, an elementary teacher in Deer River, Mich., and her three team members submitted a proposal for using technology to teach students the art and history of the Ojibwe Indians. Peterson and her colleagues felt that the school and community were not meeting the needs of the large Native American population. Native American students who experienced trouble, either academically or personally, were often written-off as unreachable. And the dropout and suicide rates among this group were extremely high. The team hoped to rectify these problems by introducing a new curriculum that enhanced the group's self-esteem and cultural pride, and helped the community understand and embrace cultural differences.

Peterson wanted to relate the Ojibwe teachings to all areas of the curriculum—helping all students, including the 25 percent who were Native American, as well as the community, become more aware of the Ojibwe culture and learn to appreciate their community's diversity. To do this, the team first had to convince the school and community to change their thinking and the way they had been "doing business" for years.

That summer, they met with the other Fellows teams at the Christa McAuliffe Institute, where they polished their project and used scenario-building to explore strategies for implementing their plans.

"The work we did at the McAuliffe Institute helped us shape our vision. It gave us the bonding time we needed to pull our plans together. And the other teachers asked us important questions that made us think our project through—they were a tremendous resource," Peterson said.

When the team returned to Deer River, they were faced with the task of getting skeptical colleagues and community members to buy in to their way of thinking. But the team was prepared. They conducted meetings and in-service sessions for the other teachers and the community to make them aware of the need for the program, and to gradually get them involved.

"There were a lot of ups and downs in implementing our program. Some of the ideas we [the team] thought were great, others thought were not so great. You have to be willing to step back and regroup—to look at what you're doing and be willing to take a slightly different approach," Peterson said.

Perhaps the greatest strength of the McAuliffe program is that it devotes a substantial amount of time to helping these teachers—many of whom already possess strong leadership and planning skills as well as an enormous amount of creativity—think organizationally about how they will implement their ideas. This is the process that often receives less attention than the work that goes into designing a project.

Like other teachers who participated in the McAuliffe Institute, scenario-building about change in their school helped Peterson and her teammates decide how to lay the groundwork needed for a smooth implementation. Their project was not only successful in integrating the curriculum and giving students a chance to study the Ojibwe culture in-depth using new technologies, it also formed a closer bond between the school and the community, enabled Native American students to take greater pride in their heritage, and helped a whole community learn to accept and celebrate cultural diversity. In 1990, the team's work was featured on the nationwide docudrama "Everyday Heroes."

Peterson offers this advice for others trying to achieve a vision: "The most important thing is to hang on to your ultimate goal and be persistent in trying to achieve that goal. We ran into many road blocks but kept reminding ourselves that our goal was to get the entire community to respect each other's diversity. That kept us going."

As NFIE says in *Images of Potential*, all scenario-building requires is "the opportunity to dream and the courage to move forward."

## Communicating the Vision

Perhaps the strongest advantage to community scenario-building is that right from the beginning, the entire learning community shapes its own vision of education, and everyone involved understands *why* changes will be made. A common vision is established, and the stakeholders are ready to accept changes that will move them toward it. If the entire learning community is not involved in the original visioning and scenario-building process, it's imperative that those who developed the vision clearly communicate it to the rest of the community.

Lack of communication is what ensnared the Belridge project. Though the principal and teachers shared a common vision, the parents did not. They didn't understand how the changes made in instruction and curriculum would eventually improve student outcomes.

When the project began, parents saw the vast amounts of new technology and the changes in curriculum as positive steps toward improving education. But two years later, after students scored slightly below the national average on the Iowa

Test of Basic Skills (no worse than scores in previous years), a handful of vocal parents led a "back to basics" campaign that demanded the school stop its restructuring efforts. Though only a few were actively denouncing the new curriculum, the other parents didn't have enough information to form a strong opposing position. The protesters eventually won, and the project was abandoned. If parents had understood the kinds of outcomes the changes would have generated over time—if they had shared the school's vision for its students—the project might have survived.

## Understanding the Nature of Change in Education

Along with communicating a vision, leaders need to make certain that communities understand the nature of change in education.

*Change takes time.*

When parents in the Belridge district saw truckloads of new technology dumped into the school in a short period of time, they assumed that improvements would happen just as fast. Change in education, especially change involving new technologies, needs to be in place a long time—perhaps five or six years—before results can be measured accurately.

*Changes in education require new ways of assessing students.*

If curriculums are going to focus on teaching students higher-order thinking skills (critical thinking, problem-solving, and reasoning), teachers need new methods of assessing student progress. Parents need to understand why curriculums are changing and why alternative assessment methods are necessary, if they are to accept the absence of traditional grading systems, report cards, and standardized tests.

*Changes in education create new roles for everyone in the learning community.*

Changes in education that contribute to the creation of a community of learners means that traditional roles are transformed. Teachers become mentors, facilitators, and managers, rather than presenters and controllers. Administrators become enablers and managers, and parents are encouraged to become active participants in educating their children. All of these groups need to understand and accept the responsibilities of their changing roles.

*Accept the possibility that some changes might fail.*

There are no formulas for successful restructuring. Each school is unique, and each student population has a different set of needs. Communities must be willing to take risks to find out what works best for their students. If a program or project doesn't work the way it was intended, learn from it, then implement something new. For successful restructuring to occur, leaders need to break the mind-set that failure is bad. Failure is not bad if it becomes part of a learning process. Leaders need to reward, not reprimand, risk-taking that may or may not be successful.

*Make ongoing change part of the vision.*

Change cannot be a one-time occurrence in schools. Futurists say that 80 percent of all jobs in the year 2000 have yet to be invented, and today's technology is likely to be obsolete within the decade. Like business and other sectors of society, education in America needs to keep changing to meet the needs of its consumers—our students. Leaders must help their communities accept change in education as a positive, ongoing process—change should be expected and accepted, not startling.

## Common Themes of Future Schools

Although each school will have a different vision, studies of schools restructured to meet the needs of students and society in the future list several common themes. Before communities embark on a restructuring journey, it's important for them to consider these recurring themes, and note how certain activities and school structures support them better than others.

Among the common themes cited by studies of efforts to restructure schools are:

- A central focus on students' characteristics and individual learning styles, e.g., self-directed, integrated, collaborative, rather than on the machinery and technology.
- A concern that technology serve all learners, including "at-risk" and disabled students, to reduce the gap between the information rich and the information poor.
- The community's vision drives all changes—especially those regarding new technologies. Technology is used as a means of achieving more in-depth and meaningful teaching and learning.
- Students applying their knowledge in purposeful activities, e.g., providing assistance to the community, working with other students on global issues, rendering relevance, practicality, and societal value to their education.
- Learning environments that extend beyond the walls of the school, often involving community members and others not traditionally associated with student learning.
- Interdisciplinary approaches to curriculum, often involving some form of teaming of teachers from different subject areas.

- High teacher expectations and belief that students are capable of solving complex problems.
- A belief in the importance of utilizing existing and emerging technologies and researching their full potential for supporting education.
- Increased responsibility for the student's own learning and the learning of others.
- The application of a mixture of technologies which extends beyond the classroom computer.
- A balance of technology-facilitated and human-facilitated learning.
- Flexible use of facilities, time, and human resources.
- Sensitivity to the development, health, and well-being of the whole learner rather than a focus limited to academic development.

Creating a vision, scenario-building, communicating the vision, and understanding the nature of change in education. These are the activities that form a foundation for the successful reshaping of America's schools, a foundation that will ensure a brighter future for tomorrow's children.

## About the Author

*Donna C. Rhodes* has served as executive director of the National Foundation for the Improvement of Education (NFIE) since 1985. Dr. Rhodes came to NFIE after serving as Executive Assistant to the President at California State University at Fullerton. She was instrumental in launching the Intergovernmental Advisory Council on Education within the US Department of Education, and served as its first Executive Director. Prior to this assignment, she was Director for the Institute for Children in the state of Kentucky. She has also been an elementary school teacher and university faculty member. Dr. Rhodes holds an interdisciplinary Ph.D. in Psychology and Education from the University of Louisville.

# 4/ Computer Support for Administrative Leadership of Schools

## William C. Bozeman

University of Central Florida


## Dennis W. Spuck

University of Houston-Clear Lake

*This chapter recounts the application of computer technology to the administration and management of educational organizations. The chapter contains three parts: the history and evolution of administrative computer applications; a summary of the results of a survey of school districts' administrative applications of computers; and consideration of technology applications for educational leadership. The chapter serves as a review of the path which computer applications have taken over the past several decades and as a foundation for analysis of present and future applications.*

## Computer Applications to School Administration: A Historical Perspective

Although administrative data processing is a familiar part of schools and educational organizations today, its history is rather brief. Many larger school districts, colleges, and universities began to use some form of electronic data processing during the mid-1950s. By the mid-1960s, data processing had become widespread in education. Financial and personnel applications (e.g., payroll, accounting, fiscal reports, etc.), inventories, class rolls, grade reporting, and master schedule generation were among early uses. In fact, business-related functions accounted for almost all computer resource utilization.

Many of the earliest computers used for educational administration were actually tabulating machines (such as the IBM 407 Accounting Machine). These machines contained a card reader, printer, and provision for functional control and instructions through a wired control panel. Usually a board was wired or programmed for a particular application (e.g., grade reporting, payroll, student lists, etc.) and then sealed for later use. Costs associated with such systems and other first generation computer technology limited the scope of educational applications to larger districts and universities.

Computers became more available in the early 1960s through lease arrangements, service bureaus, and school district consortia. Popular computers during this period were the IBM 1401 and 1410 series. The number of districts involved in computer automation of administrative functions and the number of uses increased to include bus scheduling and food service operations. Wired control panels disappeared and programming languages such as Autocoder, Symbolic Programming Systems, and COBOL became available. As telecommunications (e.g., communication between users and the district's central computer) began to be used, Autocoder was expanded to BAL (Basic Assembly Language). Though data input still relied primarily on punched cards, magnetic tape and disk storage systems enhanced system operations. More powerful systems such as the IBM 360 series during the mid-1960s and 370 series in the 1970s introduced an entirely new era of computing.

Data processing operations generally resided within the business management offices of an educational institution. Typically, this area included a manager, keypunch operators, and machine technicians. Full departments of data processing along with a director, programmers, data entry personnel, technicians, and system analysts soon emerged in educational bureaucracies. Reorganization was due to the ever-increasing complexity of automated operations as well as new hardware and technology.

The influence of these early applications of administrative computing can still be observed today in school districts, colleges, and universities. Since business-related functions comprised the majority of data processing activities, computer center personnel typically reported to a business manager or assistant superintendent for business. This bureaucratic structure continues in many educational institutions today.

The 1960s witnessed the beginning of an interest in education by computer companies including IBM, RCA, Remington Rand, Burroughs, Digital Equipment, and Honeywell. Software was written and marketed for traditional educational administrative applications such as payroll, financial accounting, inventory, and also more modern needs such as the modular student scheduling approaches, master student schedule generation, bus routing, attendance zone creation, and desegregation plans. Popularity and interest in administrative computing had become widespread by the late 1960s and early 1970s in educational institutions of all sizes. Machines continued to become more powerful and affordable while number and diversity of applications also increased.

A summary of present-day administrative computer applications in education is outlined below:

*Student Applications*
1. Student scheduling
2. Grade reporting
3. Grade and transcript information
4. Daily and summary attendance accounting
5. Student and family demographic information
6. Health records
7. Instructional management
8. Test scoring and reporting
9. Tuition and fee statements

*Personnel Applications*
1. Payroll
2. Personnel records
3. Staff assignments
4. Certification records
5. Health records
6. Tax information and W-2 reports

*Financial Applications*
1. Budget systems
2. Accounts receivable/payable
3. General ledger
4. Purchase orders
5. Salary schedule analysis

*Facilities and Equipment*
1. Space utilization and room assignment
2. Inventories
3. Maintenance scheduling
4. Energy utilization management and control

*Research and Planning Applications*
1. Budget analysis
2. Bus routing
3. Statistical analysis

    4. Test item analysis
    5. Project planning and control

*Office Applications*
    1. Word processing
    2. Filing and database systems
    3. Electronic and voice mail
    4. Desktop publishing
    5. Presentation graphics
    6. Spreadsheets

*Library Systems*
    1. Circulation
    2. Computerized catalogs
    3. On-line database searching
    4. Acquisitions and purchasing

Although this listing is not complete, it does present major applications which can be found in many educational institutions (see the bibliography for further elaboration of these applications).

The first 25 years of educational data processing offered an evolution of systems beginning with one-user tabulating machines to multiple-user timesharing systems to highly complex network environments with combinations of many different types and sizes of computers. Microcomputers, especially the IBM PC and Apple Macintosh, together with Local Area Networks dramatically changed educational management of schools and school districts in the United States.

Models of school administration systems which accompanied the advent of microcomputers precipitated a number of unanticipated changes. Changes included bureaucratic structures, financial and logistical costs of computing, staff training and technological expectations, pre-service competencies and skills, and general administrator computer literacy requirements. With the capabilities of stand-alone microcomputers, the building-level administrator was no longer completely dependent on the services of a central or district data processing manager. This independence gave administrators new opportunities for analysis of school-specific data.

Costs and logistics associated with computing changed also. The power (i.e., processor speed, memory, mass storage, etc.) of computers has increased exponentially over the past 20 years while costs have dramatically decreased. For less than $1000, a microcomputer can be purchased today which rivals the mainframe system capabilities of the past. Software and operating systems have also achieved a high degree of maturity as well as user friendliness. These new avenues to computing resources have been accompanied by changes in requisite administrator skills and competencies. For many years, technology was conspicuously absent from the educational administrator preparation curriculum. Now, technology is becoming a familiar topic in many university programs of study.

Today, computer center operations and management information systems departments are at the center of educational leadership. This should be no surprise as information is the indispensable component in all intelligent approaches to management and leadership.

## Survey of U. S. School District Automation

A recent survey conducted by The Association of School Business Officials (ASBO) documented the pervasiveness of computer use in support of the administration of schools. This study surveyed 4,129 ASBO members regarding the application of automation in their districts. The unduplicated response was 3,047 or a 74% return. The survey collected information about degree of automation, satisfaction with systems, and range of available software. Most respondents (2,066 districts or 68%) represented districts with between 1,000 and 9,999 students. Districts with 10,000 to 49,999 students comprised 6.8% of the responses and 91 districts (3%) contained over 50,000 students.

Of the total respondents, 94.8% indicated that their districts used computers to complete administrative tasks such as payroll, accounts payable, student records, etc. Sixty-two percent reported that the computer used was located in the school district. A service bureau computer was used by 16.2% of the districts, and 5.6% used a computer in another school district. The computer used for administrative tasks was not used for student instruction in 80.1% cases. Respondents were fairly equally divided with regard to type of computer used for administrative tasks: 30.4% used a mainframe, 28.9% used a minicomputer, and 31.7% used a microcomputer. IBM systems were used by the largest number (39%) of districts, having more than three times the number of its closest competitor, Digital Equipment Corporation (DEC).

With regard to how software was obtained for administrative purposes, the largest percentage (33.2%) obtained software from an outside vendor; 23.5% purchased the computer and software from the same vendor; 17.2% used in-district staff to develop software; and 9.9% used software supplied by the state or county.

Listed below, in order of frequency of mention, are administrative tasks which the districts automate:

1. Accounts Payable
2. Payroll
3. General Ledger

4. Budget Preparation
5. Check Register
6. Personnel
7. Accounts Receivable
8. Grade Reporting
9. Student Attendance
10. Master Student Scheduling
11. Student Records
12. Check Reconciliation
13. Word Processing
14. Purchasing
15. Fixed Asset Inventory
16. Inventory System
17. Spreadsheet
18. Food Services
19. Special Education
20. Teacher Scheduling
21. Negotiation
22. Student Testing Management
23. Property Control
24. Bus Routing/Transportation Management
25. Master Student Scheduling Using Rotating Schedules
26. Electronic Mail
27. Bus Fleet Maintenance
28. Bid Analysis
29. Facility Scheduling
30. Electronic Calendar
31. Library System
32. Locker Assignment
33. Automatic Absentee Call Back
34. School Maintenance Scheduling
35. Integrated Graphics
36. Boards and Councils Tracking
37. Other

## Applications to Educational Leadership

The typical day of the school administrator requires a seemingly endless series of decisions. These decisions range from rather mundane, but not unimportant, management or maintenance decisions (e.g., "Can the athletic department afford to purchase new training equipment?") to curricular-related decisions (e.g., "Should a new section of history be added to the master schedule?"). In the past, more often than not, administrators have made these decisions based on hunches, intuition, and sketchy information. Computers cannot and should not make decisions for the educational leader. They can, however, provide valuable data and information which support the decision-making process.

This section focuses on applications of computers which provide decision support, and applications which will enhance the efficiency of the administrator permitting more efficient use of time and other limited resources.

## Word Processing and Desktop Publishing

One of the most familiar and common applications of computers today is word processing and progressively desktop publishing. The combination of low-cost microcomputers and affordable letter-quality printers have made word processing an almost essential component of the school office. A few uses of these are:

1. *Faculty, student, and staff handbooks.* These tend to become dated because of the labor-intensive updating required on a periodic basis. Countless problems can be avoided by providing accurate and up-to-date procedures, rules and policies.

2. *School procedures.* Rules, regulations, and procedures, while viewed by some educators as a bureaucratic nuisance, can make the difference between an orderly, safe school and a chaotic environment. Emergency plans, evacuation routes, rainy day bus loadings, lunchroom rules, testing procedures, office referrals, etc., are all essential systems in the maintenance of an orderly, peaceful school. They must be current to be helpful, and presented in a clear, readable format.

3. *Communications and correspondence.* Good communications skills are among the most critical administrative and leadership competencies. These include common letters to the home regarding students' scholarships, school activities, honor roll acknowledgments, thank-you notes, condolences, attendance, discipline, registration, meetings, fees, curriculum, programs, events, and many other topics. Correspondence may also include faculty and staff memos and letters and communications with other schools or the central office. Often, there are only minor variances in documents, and these can be easily edited and combined with mail-merge functions of the word processor.

4. *Forms.* Schools, like most institutions, require a myriad of forms. They vary from simple data-gathering instruments and surveys to student performance contracts to legal contracts for services. Often minor edits can alleviate much time and work when using a form for a different purpose.

5. *Reports and other educational documents.* Because education is an information/knowledge-based enterprise, considerable resources are contributed to the production of reports and documentation (district and state department

reports, accreditation agency documents, school improvement and strategic plans, etc.).

An added advantage inherent in all of the above applications of word processing is the reduction or elimination of paper files. Documents stored in electronic form can be easily retrieved for future reference and review. The reduction in space and suitable storage areas for paper documents can also contribute to a more efficient management system. Desktop publishing extends the word processing capability to access a greater array of fonts; include photographs, illustrations, and graphs; and create columns and formats which duplicate those associated with professional printers, thus providing camera ready copy of the highest quality.

## *Spreadsheets*

Electronic spreadsheets (e.g., *Lotus* 1-2-3, *Quattro*, *Excel*) have become almost synonymous with microcomputers. In fact, it has been hypothesized that the popularity of spreadsheets was the primary stimulus for the success of the microcomputer industry. Spreadsheets permit the entering of data (text, numbers, and formulae) into a grid or matrix. Then they can be used and processed in calculations, projections, statistical analysis, and graphical display.

Spreadsheet programs first appeared in 1979 with the *VisiCalc* program for the Apple II microcomputer. The reaction and acceptance was beyond anyone's imagination and it quickly became a best-selling program. In 1983, *VisiCalc*'s popularity was overtaken by *Lotus* 1-2-3. Lotus was similar in many respects to *Visicalc* and other spreadsheets, but distinguished by the incorporation of graphics features and database management capabilities.

Given below are just a few possible spreadsheet applications to school management:

1. *Budgets.* School, department, athletic, and lunchroom budgets are ultimately the responsibility of the school administrator. Spreadsheets permit the asking of "What if ... ?" questions as possible revenues and expenditures are considered. The ability to immediately recalculate a budget given different parameters or assumptions can result in a more efficient and productive use of valuable time as well as improved fiscal management.

2. *Grade analysis.* Examination and inspection of grades as reported by student demographics, teachers, departments, and grade levels may reveal trends worthy of further investigation. Significant deviations by gender or ethnicity, for example, could suggest areas of the curriculum in need of attention or possible needs for faculty development.

3. *Enrollment, attendance, and FTE analysis.* Assisting in the monitoring and reporting of attendance records, attendance records management can

generate attendance reports and absence lists, and provide a database for analysis of attendance patterns, automated telephone follow-up of absences, and reporting of summary enrollment information for school, district and state needs.

4. *Free and reduced lunch calculations.* Spreadsheet systems can assist schools by maintaining files of students who qualify for free or reduced-fee lunch and generate reports of numbers and usage of this program, as required by governmental agencies.

5. *Salary schedules.* The salary schedule and number of teachers on each step of the schedule can be combined to provide school and district personnel calculations of costs. Such capability is useful not only for computing the cost of the schedule currently in use, but in simulating costs of salary schedule alternatives as might be considered by school administrators.

6. *General ledger.* The logging of income and expenditures can be documented through an automated general ledger. Summary totals can be generated as needed to track cash flow and to support revenue management.

## Database Systems

Database management systems and computer-based filing systems have been among the more important administrative applications of computers for years. Essentially, such systems allow storage organization, retrieval, and management. Below are selected applications which may enhance effectiveness and efficiency of the school administrator:

1. *Faculty and staff assignments.* Database systems can assist in making and retrieving information on faculty and staff assignments. This information can be used to summarize personnel utilization and for estimating human resource needs.

2. *Faculty and student lists and directories.* Schools must maintain numerous lists and generate reports on the location and involvement of students and teachers in classes, clubs, busses, sports activities, field trips, etc., as well as maintain student and personnel files.

3. *Discipline referrals.* As a part of the comprehensive set of information collected on students, most schools find it necessary to maintain data on disciplinary referrals and the dispensation of these referrals. Such historical information is helpful in making future decisions related to discipline, as well as documenting trends and cumulative records of behavior.

4. *Facility utilization.* Schools are large and complex organizations, not only in the numbers of people involved, but also in the utilization of physical space. Database systems can assist administrators in ensuring that available space is utilized efficiently through the generation of space utilization reports.

5. *Locker and key management.* The assignment of students to lockers and keeping track of key codes or combinations associated with individual students

and lockers can be a time-consuming and difficult task. Database systems can assist with the maintenance of information which associates students, lockers, and keys.

6. *Automobile registration and parking.* Similar to the preceding application, another collection of student related information is the logging and assignment of students and their cars to parking places and parking permit numbers.

7. *Equipment inventory and maintenance schedules.* Schools contain vast quantities of equipment which must be inventoried and in many cases regularly maintained. Database systems can assist in keeping track of the location, description, serial numbers, inventory numbers, and value of equipment, and also can generate maintenance schedules and logs as required.

The above lists and descriptions of possible applications of word processing and desktop publishing, spreadsheet, and database applications are not meant to be exhaustive, but illustrative. Indeed the power of these systems is in their flexibility in meeting the needs of administrators and schools and in conforming to the decision and information requirements of their individual users.

## The Future of Administrative Technology Applications

Several trends seem to be emerging as we look toward the future. The availability of reasonably priced and user friendly hardware and software is leading to a greater use of integrated applications and database systems; this availability permits more integrated approaches to managing schools in both the business functions and the instructional uses of technology.

Computing trends in education indicate a definite merger between instructional and administrative data processing. The ASBO Survey, discussed above, indicated a common evolution in the use of educational administrative applications across school districts of different sizes. Most districts did, in fact, begin the use of computer technology in the business office, then spread into the student records, personnel and materials management applications. In parallel, most school systems have become increasingly involved in instructional computing at the classroom and building level.

Increased "computer awareness" and "technology comfort" at the building administrator and teacher levels resulting from the instructional computing revolution, are prerequisites to the eventual merger of instructional and administrative technology. This factor, combined with the growing trend towards more school-based management and greater accountability for student performance at the building level, creates a natural synergistic effect for the merger of these technologies. Furthermore, the merger may well be a survival mechanism for school based staff.

It is predicted that the emphasis on data-based decision-making in schools will be implemented and augmented by many school districts in the United

States within this decade. More importantly, the use of computer technology as a decision support tool will be the new wave of technological applications in education. By the turn of the century, a principal using a computer to diagnose and resolve student instructional problems could be as commonplace as today's accountant using a calculator or a personal computer. Exciting times and much hard work are ahead, however, if data are to become a school resource and computer technology is to become a tool for improving the quality of instructional decision-making.

# References

Bozeman, W. C. & House, J. E. (1988, February). Microcomputers in education: The second decade. *THE Journal, 15*(6), 82–86.

Bozeman, W. C. & Raucher, S. M. (1991). Application of computer technology to educational administration in the United States of America. *Journal of Research on Computing in Education, 24*(1), 62–77.

Bozeman, W. C. & Spuck, D. W. (1991). Technology competence training for educational leaders. *Journal of Research on Computing in Education, 23*(4), 514–529.

Cheever, D. S. Jr., Coburn, P., DiGiammarino, F., Kelman, P., Lowd, B. T., Naiman, A., Sayer, G. A., Temkin, K. & Zimmerman, I. K. (1986). *School Administrator's Guide to Computers in Education.* Reading, MA: Addison-Wesley.

Gustafson, T. J. (1985). *Microcomputers and Educational Administration.* Englewood Cliffs, NJ: Prentice-Hall.

Kearsley, G. (1988). What should today's school administrators know about computers? *THE Journal, 15*(3), 65–69.

Loughary, J. W. (1966). *Man-Machine Systems in Education.* New York: Harper & Row.

Miller, H. (1988). *An Administrator's Manual for the Use of Microcomputers in the Schools.* Englewood Cliffs, NJ: Prentice-Hall.

Mimms, T. & Poirot, J. (1984). Computer competencies for school administrators. *International Council on Computing in Education SIG Bulletin I,* 19–22.

Pogrow, S. (1985). Administrative uses of computers: What is the ideal system? What are the trends? *NASSP Bulletin, 69*(485), 45–53.

Raucher, S. M. (1990, May). A school-based instructional monitoring system. *School Business Affairs,* 6–9.

Richards, C. E. (1989). *Microcomputer Applications for Strategic Management in Education.* New York: Longman.

Samuels, M. H. & Holtzapple-Toxey, L. (1987). Perceived needs of school administrators for computer training: A study. *Computers in the Schools, 4*(2), 71–78.

Spuck, D. W. & Bozeman, W. C. (1988). Training school administrators in computer use. *Journal of Research on Computing in Education, 21*(2), 229–239.

Weal, E. (1992). Using technology to enhance decision-making. *Apple Education Review,* (1), 2–3.

## About the Authors

*William C. Bozeman* received his Ph.D. in Educational Administration from the University of Wisconsin and currently serves as Professor of Educational Leadership and Chair of the Department of Educational Services at the University of Central Florida.

*Dennis W. Spuck* is Dean of the School of Education at the University of Houston-Clear Lake, where he also is Professor of Educational Leadership and Foundations. He received his Ph.D. from the Claremont Graduate School.

# Part II: Examples

Part I outlined a number of issues and questions about the nature of educational technology leadership. The chapters in Part II present a series of case studies of educational technology leadership at different levels ranging from individual teachers to national policy. These chapters capture the complexity and complications of implementing technology in a single school or an entire state or country.

In Chapter 5, Ferris and Roberts document the stories of five teachers who became recognized as technology leaders in their schools. Each case study includes: (1) the first encounter with technology, (2) emergence as a leader, (3) obstacles encountered and overcome, (4) school-wide acceptance, and (5) advice for improving the use of technology in schools. Over the past two decades, thousands of teachers have gone through similar experiences as the five teachers described in this chapter in their quest to be better educators and to take advantage of what technology has to offer.

Chapter 6, by Furlong and Rolley, elaborates on the concept of "vision" in the context of two major technology projects: SeniorNet and Apple Core. SeniorNet is a national organization with thousands of members that encourages computer use by older adults. The project started with a simple idea—to see if senior citizens were interested in using computers—and this idea grew into a full-scale social innovation. Apple Core began as the solo effort of one principal to help other private school administrators learn to use computers, and evolved into a national support network. In both of these projects, a vision was nurtured well enough to grow into a very successful application of educational technology.

In Chapter 7, Branson and Hirumi outline the design of a technology-based model for education in the state of Florida. The authors argue that systematic change is needed in order for technology to have a significant and long-term impact in education. The Florida Schoolyear 2000 model is an attempt to provide new structures, procedures, and processes for implementing technology in all Florida schools. The model encompasses curriculum, instruction, student and family services, assessment and information management, human resource development, management operations, logistics, evaluation, and research. Leadership in the SY2000 model is highly participatory in nature.

Collis & Moonen deal with a very important leadership issue in Chapter 8: the transition from a special project to systemwide integration. This issue is examined in the context of information technology in the Dutch educational system with particular focus on the role of school administrators. The nature of leadership in the special project phase of technology is compared to the leadership requirements of systemwide implementation. The case study allows us to examine the transition process in detail, and to study how leadership qualities are manifest in real settings.

Robinson provides an account in Chapter 9 of leadership at the national level. He describes the evolution of information technology in the English educational system. Government policies and legislation have played a prominent role in the development of technology in English schools, and have resulted in a national curriculum for information technology. Changes in the roles and responsibilities of teachers, coordinators, and administrators due to the implementation of the information technology curriculum are discussed with particular attention to the nature of leadership required at different levels of the school system.

# 5/ Teachers as Technology Leaders: Five Case Studies

## Angeline Ferris and Nancy Roberts

Lesley College

*Teachers represent the front line of technology leadership. This chapter presents five case studies of teachers who are recognized as technology leaders in their schools. Each case study describes their: first encounter with technology, emergence as a leader, obstacles encountered, school-wide use, and advice for improving technology. A set of common characteristics of successful implementations emerges from these case studies.*

## Introduction

In this chapter the authors try to understand what makes teachers *technology leaders*. Because of our graduate program in Computers in Education, begun in 1979, we had a pool of several hundred alumni and other teachers from which to select. We selected these teachers because they represent both elementary and secondary education as well as urban, suburban, and independent schools. Over the last 15 years the authors have worked with each of these people and know and admire them as leaders in bringing technology to their schools. The authors developed a lengthy questionnaire to augment this working knowledge.

The interviews administered over the course of a summer suggest that outside school support, administrative support, and the awareness by all that change in a school is slow are all critical factors in creating and maintaining technology leaders. Additional money can indeed help, but as shown by one of the situations, it is not the area of greatest leverage to sustain leadership. In addition it is interesting to note the similarity of the advice given by each of the teachers.

Each interview report is divided into six parts that reflect the series of questions the authors compiled for the interviews:

- background information such as education;
- a description of the teacher's first encounter with technology;
- when and how the teacher emerged as a leader;
- obstacles each has encountered to using technology;
- a description of each teacher's school-wide uses of technology; and
- advice for improving use of technology.

# Frank Draper

## *Background*

Frank graduated from California State University at Fullerton in 1974 with a degree in biological sciences. Marrying soon after college, Frank and his wife moved to Minnesota. Frank's first job, as a park naturalist, was essentially a teaching job. Because he loved it, Frank decided to go back to school for his teaching credentials, earning a second bachelor's degree at St. Cloud College.

## *First Encounter with Technology*

During his seven years teaching in Minnesota, Frank taught secondary level life and physical sciences, biology, and ecology. He preferred working with older students because of their increased sophistication. He most enjoyed teaching ecology. In 1984 his school bought some Commodore computers. Having seen an Apple computer in his daughter's classroom the year before, Frank realized how much easier it was to use the new desktop computers than the computers he had used in his FORTRAN course in college. In response to a request from the chair of the mathematics department, he volunteered to try the new machines. His initial uses were to animate chemistry lectures, for remediation, and to integrate MECC (Minnesota Educational Computer Consortium) simulations into his ecology and life science classes.

Frank became intrigued with the students' reactions to simulations, as they created stories around the simulation topics. Using the simulation, *Oh Deer*, the students managed a deer herd and met with all the social conflicts that were going on in Minnesota then, such as "What should be the optimal deer size to avoid overgrazing and neighbor disturbance?" The simulation software led the students beyond rote memorization. As they took on the roles in the simulation, they started "reading between the lines," extending the simulation issues, and became more cognizant of their own beliefs. The students began to understand that, depending on the point of view, everyone was "right." Having learned BASIC, Frank tried writing his own simulations, but he never finished any.

Frank tried to get other teachers in his schools involved with computers, using the argument that simulations help students build their own understandings of situations and events. He found his colleagues generally frightened or put off by the machines. Training was available on a voluntary basis but most of the other teachers chose not to attend. He managed to get one chemistry, one physics, and one social studies teacher involved. The social studies teacher ran the whole junior high class through the program *Oregon Trail.*

## Emergence as a Leader

In 1986 the Drapers moved to Tucson, Arizona. Here Frank taught middle school life science as well as several science electives. He began taking courses at the University of Arizona for license continuation and eventually earned a master's degree in education. In the spring of 1988 he and a co-teacher, Mark Swanson, were looking for ways to improve their courses. They had been experimenting with using video images to enhance direct instruction. In fact, they had won a Macintosh computer at Arizona State University's Microcomputers in Education Conference for combining a videodisc with an Apple II computer to augment their lectures.

At this time the Catalina Foothills School District was soliciting community approval to issue a bond for a new high school. At a neighborhood meeting, Gordon Brown, Professor Emeritus from MIT and former head of the Electrical Engineering Department, became intrigued with the superintendent's educational vision. After the meeting, Gordon talked to the superintendent about systems thinking, and a new, iconic-based simulation language called STELLA. The superintendent directed Gordon to Frank and Mark. During their first meeting, Gordon showed them STELLA. Remembering this first meeting, Frank commented, "I can imagine our eyes must have popped. This was just what we were looking for. 'We can use this!' were our first words. Now, instead of trying to absorb the collection of isolated facts in lectures, our students could examine relationships and learn through direct manipulation of systems" (Draper, 1989). Frank borrowed the software and the book, *Introduction to Computer Simulation: A System Dynamics Modeling Approach* (Roberts *et al.*, 1983) and within a few weeks was using it in class.

Gordon's enthusiasm and Frank's receptivity prompted Gordon to find support for Frank's efforts. Through High Performance Systems, the company that publishes STELLA, Gordon learned that there was a training session for teachers that summer in Stanford, California. The Educational Testing Service (ETS) sponsored the training in conjunction with a project to integrate systems thinking into six San Francisco area high schools. Frank attended. "By September [1988], after several days discussion with Mark Swanson about the workshop, we were ready to use systems dynamics and systems thinking in our classrooms. We made the critically important decision that instead of teaching systems as an adjunct unit somewhere in the year, we would present our science topics as the systems they truly are. Our students would learn about systems through science content" (Draper, 1989).

In the fall, Frank started using STELLA with his one Macintosh computer and an Orange Grove Middle School class of 22 students. Frank and Mark then devised a classroom management technique that they call multitasking, allowing them to cycle about 200 students every two weeks through a unit that gives each student a chance to use a STELLA simulation. Students, in teams of four, are assigned to a one period task. During a two-week period each team works at several different tasks related to solving an actual science-based problem. One of the first problems the class tackled was "designing a new state park within a budget and prescribed mission" (Draper & Swanson, 1990, p. 211).

Frank described the outcomes of their initial work: "Since October 1988 our classrooms have undergone an amazing transformation. Not only are we covering more material than just the required curriculum, but we are covering it faster and the students are learning more useful material than ever before. 'Facts' are now anchored to meaning through the dynamic relationships they have with each other. In our classroom students shift from being passive receptacles to being active learners. They are not taught about science per se, but learn how to acquire and use knowledge. Our jobs have shifted from dispensers of information to producers of environments which allow students to learn as much as possible" (Draper, 1989).

Continuing as an active supporter of Frank's efforts, Gordon next went to Apple Computer for a donation of Macintosh computers. This resulted in Frank's class becoming part of Apple's Classrooms of Tomorrow program as an Experimental Learning Center. A class set of Macintosh computers arrived in the spring of 1989. Gordon also went to the Waters Foundation in Framingham, Massachusetts for financial support. With an initial $30,000 from Waters, Frank was able to hire a part-time teacher to give Mark and Frank time to create more STELLA simulations for class use as well as to hire trainers from High Performance Systems. The whole staff at the Orange Grove Middle School received two days of training in system thinking and STELLA in the fall of '89 and again in the spring of '90. During this school year, Frank and Mark reorganized the entire eighth grade science curriculum in terms of systems. The core of the curriculum was the life sciences, but also included were many other sciences as well.

The new principal at the middle school became quite excited about the possibilities of applying system dynamics philosophy to school management. Frank encouraged this interest by continuously supplying her with appropriate readings, which she then shared with the whole staff. During the summer of 1990, Frank attended the International System Dynamics Conference in Massachusetts. Here he met Peter Senge who gave him a copy of his new book, *The Fifth Discipline*. Sharing the book with his principal, they found it gave the school staff a common language with which to create a collective systems vision.

By the spring of '90, it was clear that the whole staff needed much more extensive systems training than the four days thus far scheduled. Moreover, partial release time for Frank and Mark did not work well. The students never accepted the part-time teacher as their "real teacher." Another proposal was submitted to the Waters Foundation for $150,000 per year for three years. When funded, it allowed Frank to change his role from a classroom teacher to a mentor teacher. In this new position Frank did not have responsibility for any classes, so he could do additional systems training for the middle school staff as well as work with teachers individually and in teams to develop new curriculum and revise older materials. This second Waters grant allowed the school staff to structure itself into grade level interdisciplinary teacher teams. The teams continued to revise both how school was conducted and the curriculum with their growing systems vision.

The most significant changes during the first year were:

- The teachers started taking a systematic look at what each other was teaching—they tried to meet in teams each week to plan an integrated curriculum, keeping the big picture always in mind,
- Almost all problems, both individual student problems and school problems, are handled by the teams rather than by the principal,
- The number of disciplinary problems decreased—the students said that the school work was so much more interesting they did not have time to get into trouble,
- The time schedule became much more flexible—if a teacher needed more time for a particular period, it was easy to accomplish,
- The teachers' roles shifted from evaluators to coaches.

Some of the teachers tried integrating systems thinking into their courses by using causal-loop diagrams and STELLA simulations. This approach enriched their work with non-computer simulations such as mock trials, a mock senate, and even a mock city. The teachers called their new approach to curriculum student-centered learning. However, the traditional middle school courses were still maintained and the teachers still chose the main topics of study. Change continued during the 1991–92 school year. Many more teachers integrated causal-loop diagrams, a system dynamics problem-solving tool, into their courses. An eighth grade literature teacher introduced flow diagrams, one step closer to mathematical modeling, to his class. Topics of study became more interrelated from course to course. Teachers came to Frank to talk about how particular structures they were considering setting up in their class would affect student behavior and student engagement. One teacher told Frank that systems thinking helped him understand that his actions provoked a student behavior he did not want. By the end of the year students could readily give examples of how the systems thinking curriculum carried over into their everyday life. The students particularly mentioned tools, such as causal-loop diagramming, and skills such as being able to understand other people's perspective and analyzing hypotheses, as being universally useful.

By the spring of 1991, Frank was getting five or six calls a day asking questions about the school's activities. He put together a packet of materials for distribution and received a small grant to make a video tape explaining the school's evolving philosophy. These steps helped, but Frank decided a conference would be another technique for sharing Orange Grove Middle School's work with a wider audience. The conference attracted 230 persons and half of the middle school staff participated. Their presentations provided the teachers with the need and motivation to take a hard look at what they were doing. During the '91–'92 school year, those who participated shared their presentations with the teachers who did not attend the conference. The Catalina Foothills School district hosted a second conference in June of 1993.

Frank attributes important differences in his school to the systems thinking experiment, even though, at first glance, the school might look like most other middle schools. For the teachers these differences include:

- Things that used to be private—activities that would take place behind a teacher's closed door—are now discussed openly. Failures are talked about and teachers' seek help from colleagues.
- Teachers' thinking and discussions are now at several different levels making a much more professional environment. Now when teachers evaluate a lesson they may relate it to their curriculum and learning theories, not just whether "it worked."
- Teachers are much more likely to think about the whole student, to find out what is going on in other classes, and to look for patterns of behavior, rather than just consider the student in isolation.
- The idea of scope and sequence now makes much more sense because teachers are taking a more holistic view of curriculum. Teachers are also taking a longitudinal view of curriculum by making their plans based on what came before and what is coming after. This is supported by posting each team's year curriculum and each quarter's activities in the team's meeting area.

For students the teachers have observed:

- A much higher overall interest in school—as evident by the students' conversations which are far more content oriented.
- A greater interest in the curriculum because it focuses on real world situations.

- The students enthusiasm using simulations. They become very involved in the content of the simulation. One situation simulated a farm where the student teams had to decide such things as what crops to grow, when to harvest, and how much insecticides to use. A slower student became star of the week because his father had been a farmer. His interest in school remained with him for the rest of the school year.
- This approach as "especially appropriate for at-risk students, such as minorities and special needs children. They become active participants in their education, not passive vessels" (Draper and Swanson, 1990, p. 212).
- Students talking "directly to each other... I did not have to filter the information from one student back to the rest of the class" (Hopkins, 1991, p. 4). Frank stresses the staff still has a lot to learn, especially how to make these successes more widespread to affect all the students.

For the next few years Frank will work at the new high school as a mentor teacher. His tasks are similar to those at the middle school. His challenge is to figure out how best to capitalize on the system thinking skills the students bring with them from Orange Grove. He is eager to see if the students are able to use their new skills when appropriate. As the students mature, they might be able to construct mathematical models on their own. They would then truly have a full range of skills to do scientific investigations.

## Obstacles to Using Technology

One major obstacle is teaching with a limited resource. Before Orange Grove became part of the Apple Classrooms of Tomorrow (ACOT) program, which provided computers for every classroom, Frank found the curriculum really got "jerked around" with too few computers. However, becoming an ACOT school put teachers under much pressure. They feel they need immediately to do something "whiz bang" with the technology. Teachers therefore create artificial needs for the computers, which increases the tensions. Another problem is communicating to the parents that a non-familiar curriculum can succeed. Frank has had to show the parents that the necessary content is being learned when students use simulations in science and spreadsheets in mathematics. Parents ask to see the teacher's syllabus when curriculum begins to look too different.

Frank finds his administration always very supportive. He always invites his principal into his room soon after he tries something new. He feels this is especially true with technology because of the time it takes to develop a level of comfort. Frank's advice is it is always easier to explain what you are doing rather than ask permission to do it.

## School-wide Uses of Technology

Technology is beginning to be naturally integrated into the learning of the school. In one class the students are using a board simulation, *Fish Banks*, to try to control the quality, quantity, and variety of fish. The students enter each round's simulation data into spreadsheet software on a networked computer. The data goes to the server which combines the data from each team and sends the aggregated data back to each computer on the network. In this way the computer does all the number crunching and the students spend their time on strategy discussions and policy-making. One of the focuses of seventh grade science is geology. To make the subject more relevant, the students use a mining company simulation. First they have to find the best potential site for copper. Once the mine is in operation, the teams decide such things as the level of productivity and how much money to put back into research and development. Another activity of the simulation is bidding at auction on new mining leases. The simulation has a supply and demand index that feeds back into the price of copper, allowing the simulation to act very much like the mining sector of our economy.

Frank has created simulations for several teachers, but only when the computer allows the teachers to do something that the students could not do otherwise—usually involving interaction with data. Other examples of Orange Grove's uses of technology include:

- a simulation to accompany the study of *Animal Farm* for an eighth grade literature class;
- a seventh grade social studies simulation to understand the differences in food supplies for developed versus underdeveloped countries;
- a spreadsheet-based simulation in mathematics to teach about money management;
- a sixth grade social studies simulation where teams of students act as people from different countries bartering goods such as food and weapons;
- the physical education teacher digitizes images of students engaged in sports so the students can analyze their tennis swing or volley ball serve; and
- students use hypertext for creating reports.

Even with all this variety of technology uses, only about two of the seven teachers at each grade level have made marked progress on integrating technology into their classrooms. However, in the new Catalina Foothills High School, all teachers have a high level of comfort with technology. The school is part of the Essential Schools Coalition. It uses system thinking as an organizing philosophy, and is totally integrated with technology.

## *Advice for Improving Use of Technology*

Teachers need to be the motivator for using technology. Another person can help a teacher recognize needs that already exist, but reasons to use technology should never be invented. Once a teacher becomes interested, the technology-related support needs to be ongoing, with many opportunities to practice using the selected technology. Support is best from another teacher or at least a person who has been a classroom teacher. The support person should begin by understanding the teacher's ideas about teaching, match technology to the teacher's philosophy, and then help the teacher to get his or her hands "dirty" as soon as possible.

# Janis Rennie

## *Background*

Janis started considering a teaching career while she was in elementary school. Janis was particularly inspired by her fourth grade teacher whom she idolized. As she progressed through school, other teachers encouraged her to become an educator. Looking back, Janis feels that the interest these teachers took in her was positive, but limiting, as she was never encouraged to pursue other careers. Her physics teacher urged her to teach physics, but never mentioned other careers in physics. Janis' family also thought she should pursue a career in teaching. To them it was one of the best career options open to women.

Janis attended Skidmore College and graduated with a degree in Elementary Education and a minor in English. She had planned to minor in mathematics, but a bad experience discouraged her. As a result of a freshman placement test Janis was assigned to the advanced instead of the regular calculus class. Since she did not have the prerequisite material the class was difficult and discouraging. At the same time, a "good" experience in an English class convinced her to minor in English. Janis has a master's degree in Reading from Suffolk University, a Certificate of Advanced Graduate Study (CAGS) from Lesley College in Curriculum and Instruction with a concentration in computers, and has completed the additional course work needed for administrative certification. Janis began teaching courses for Lesley College after completing her CAGS. She helped develop the course Integrating Computers into the School Curriculum that she teaches both at the Cambridge campus and at other Lesley locations throughout the country. Being an adjunct faculty member enriches Janis' work. Janis is able to stay current in the latest hardware and software through use of the Lesley facilities. In addition, Janis is in contact with Lesley faculty members and students from many regions of the country.

For the past 21 years Janis worked for the public school system in Chelsea, Massachusetts, one of the poorest small city school systems in the country. Janis held many different positions within the Chelsea School System. She taught first grade, fourth grade, remedial reading at the high school, served as the curriculum coordinator for the elementary schools, and was Acting Director of Chapter I. Janis felt it was important for her to change positions frequently to "stay fresh." Of all these grade levels, the elementary age students are her favorite. After 21 years, Janis resigned her position in Chelsea to become the principal of the K–4 elementary school in Lynnfield, Massachusetts.

### First Encounter with Technology

Janis first became interested in computers while she was teaching reading in Chelsea High School. A few teachers at the high school were working in BASIC. Because their work intrigued Janis, she decided to get some first-hand experience with computers. She took a course in BASIC at a local Radio Shack store and followed it with a course in Logo offered by the Boston Museum of Science. It was the course in Logo that inspired her to continue working with computers. The philosophy behind Logo captivated her. She decided that she wanted to continue exploring educational uses of computers by taking courses in Lesley College's Computers in Education program. She started with the Computer Literacy course to experience first-hand the program's philosophy. Finding the course interesting and appropriate, Janis enrolled in the CAGS program.

### Emergence as a Leader

Janis immediately applied the knowledge from her course work at Lesley to her job in Chelsea. Her final project for the Literacy course was to redesign a computer club for the high school. Over the next couple of years a small core of computer-using teachers emerged in the high school. Janis, the librarian, and others began to explore ways to use computers. With the support of the principal, these teachers offered in-service workshops to the other faculty. Gradually the group of computer-using teachers expanded.

In 1986, Janis changed positions and became the curriculum coordinator for the four elementary schools in Chelsea. In this new position, Janis had the opportunity to work closely with the director of state and federal grants for the city. Through their efforts, they were able to furnish each school with computer equipment (Apple IIe's) and to provide teachers with in-service training.

### Obstacles to Using Technology

Janis feels that making good purchasing decisions is critical. Computers are not always the answer. With one grant the school bought large-screen monitors and overlay projection panels. This allows teachers with one computer in their classroom to teach a whole class lesson. To Janis this is more important than buying a few more computers.

## School-wide Uses of Technology

Janis' work as the curriculum coordinator put her in a perfect position to influence the use of computers in the elementary schools. Integration into the curriculum rather than teaching computers as a separate subject is the focus of her work. The "Tool" use of the computer is emphasized with such software as word processing, graphing, and making timelines. One school acquired enough equipment to set up a writing lab. The lab is staffed by a writing teacher who is comfortable using the technology. Classroom teachers accompany their students to the writing lab. The two teachers, working together, prove to be an effective combination. The writing done in the lab is well coordinated with the classroom curriculum. A bonus was that the classroom teachers are much more comfortable using the technology. Another school set up an after-school club. This club works as a partnership where students and their parents come together to work on the computers.

Since Boston University took over the administration of the Chelsea Schools in 1989, there has been a major push to teach basic skills. Although there was much disagreement, Boston University installed a Josten's Integrated Learning System in each school. The purpose of these systems—to teach basic skills—is a decided departure from the integrated approach to technology characteristic of the earlier years. Janis is hopeful that students can profit from both approaches. Many teachers are, however, using the Integrated Learning Systems to teach writing. The teachers in Chelsea continue to show more ownership of the technology, and their uses of technology do not always follow the "basic skills" approach being advocated by Boston University. Janis cautions that if the only experience students get with computers is "drill and practice," then the ILS systems are doing the kids a real disservice. If, on the other hand, the drill and practice is done on the computers, then theoretically the teachers are available to focus more on higher-level thinking skills.

## Advice for Improving Use of Technology

Janis offers the following advice  to schools implementing technology in elementary schools:

- The use of the computers must be linked to the curriculum.
- The placement of the computers is important. She believes that labs or clusters of computers are more effective for most teachers than the one computer classroom.
- Teachers need colleagues that can help them when they have problems.

- Training must be on-going and linked to the current needs. Janis has the opportunity to follow her own advice in her new job as an elementary principal in another Massachusetts community.

## Linda Carey and Marthanne Pressey

*Background*

The Killam School in Reading, Massachusetts is an outstanding elementary school ( K–5). The school is known for its excellent writing program and for its whole language approach to language arts. The Carnegie Foundation gave the Killam School a grant for a restructuring project so that the school can become a "community of learners." Teachers and parents are given time to work collaboratively on developing curriculum. Computers are integrated throughout the school. This has taken a number of years to accomplish, starting ten years ago when a small group of teachers became interested in computers and their role in education. Linda Carey and Marthanne (Marty) Pressey were two of the first to become involved with technology.

Linda Carey began teaching after graduating from Boston State College in 1962, where she majored in education with a minor in science. Linda never seriously considered a career other than teaching. She said, "It was a time when you (referring to women) were a teacher, nurse, or secretary." Since Linda loved school, she found it an easy decision to become a teacher. She taught sixth grade for four years and then resigned to raise her own family. While at home she took courses to obtain special education certification. She felt that special education certification would help her secure a teaching position in a tight job market. In 1976, after ten years as a home maker, Linda returned to work part-time as a resource room teacher. Four years later she became a full-time classroom teacher. Linda has taught first, second, fourth, and sixth grades. Her present position as a fourth grade teacher is her favorite. She has taught at the Killam School since 1984.

Marty Pressey is a special needs teacher at the Killam School. She has been a friend of Linda's for many years. Marty attended Ohio Wesleyan, transferred to Wheelock College in Boston, and graduated with a degree in Early Childhood Education in 1963. Teaching also seemed like a logical career choice to Marty. Her mother was a teacher and she, too, stated it was one of the "few avenues open to women" at that time. Marty holds a master's degree in Reading and Language from the University of Lowell. Marty also holds certification in special needs. Over the years, she has taught a variety of positions including: third grade, preschool, and reading.

In her current position, Marty works closely with all the classroom teachers. Most of the assistance given to special education students at Killam is done in the regular classroom rather than in a pull-out program. In addition to her work at the Killam, Marty teaches graduate special education courses at Lesley College in Cambridge, Massachusetts, where she has been an adjunct faculty member for 12 years. She is a firm believer that her work at Lesley and her work at the Killam School complement each other. The research and teaching that Marty does at Lesley has a direct impact on her view of the curriculum at Killam. Her work with elementary students enables her to bring vivid examples into her classes at Lesley.

Marty first became interested in computers around 1980. After finishing her master's degree, she took a few courses in computers. She signed up for an Introduction to Computers course, because, as she explained, "I just like to try new things." Her husband purchased an Apple computer to use at home. At the suggestion of some Lesley faculty members, Marty read *Mindstorms* by Seymour Papert. The book had a deep influence on her views about computers and education, and as a result she took a week-long Logo course.

## First Encounter with Technology

Linda found it hard to remember exactly how she became involved with computers. She bought a home computer, a TRS 80, while her children were in elementary school. She took a course in BASIC programming around 1980. She also took several workshops that were mandated by the school system. A required Logo workshop was "a real disappointment" to Linda. Later, however, she became a firm believer in Logo and the philosophy behind the language. Around this time, Linda considered pursuing a master's degree. It seemed logical to focus her work around technology since she sensed that computers were "important" and were not just a fad. Linda enrolled in a program at the University of Lowell and in 1989 received a master's degree in Curriculum Development with a computer strand.

A small group of teachers interested in technology started to form at the Killam School. The group included Linda, Marty, the librarian, and several other teachers. This group started using the Apple II equipment the district had purchased. They talked about their work and shared ideas. They helped each other with problems and provided assistance to their colleagues. Both Marty and Linda feel that this group really spurred them on to experiment more and more with the technology. They believe that the placement of the computer lab in the Killam library is a positive factor in promoting computer use in the building. The library is in an open area of the school and is central to the classrooms. Teachers walking by the area see motivated students working on a variety of tasks from word processing to Logo and often stop and talk to students or colleagues.

In the spring of 1989, Marty saw an advertisement in the *Boston Globe* describing a project of the Massachusetts Institute of Technology (MIT) Media Lab under the direction of Seymour Papert. The project, Science and Whole

Learning, was seeking schools to participate. Marty and Linda were excited about the possibility of being involved. Impressed by Dr. Papert's work in Logo they felt that their participation in the project would greatly enrich their teaching. Together with a teacher from Lawrence, they wrote a proposal. Lawrence is an old mill town, once prosperous but, now feeling the loss of many industries. The proposal argued that students from these two diverse communities would profit from sharing their science work. Their proposal was one of seven accepted. The teachers believe that their proposal was approved because of the collaboration between the inner city school in Lawrence and an innovative suburban school.

Marty and Linda spent three weeks in the summer of 1989 attending an intensive workshop at MIT including *LogoWriter*, *LegoLogo*, and exposure to all sorts of new technology. In the fall, Linda and Marty began teaching Logo with new vigor. They arranged their schedule so that they taught Logo the last period every Monday. A graduate student from MIT was assigned to help them. This graduate student participated in the Monday classes and then stayed on after school to work with the teachers. Both teachers feel that it was critical to have this technical help available on a regular basis. The project ended with a one-week workshop the following summer. Despite the end of the funding, approximately 30 of the original 45 teachers involved chose to keep working together. In the summer of 1991, the group met for a one-week workshop. Seymour Papert had secured a grant to fund this endeavor. The group, which renamed itself the "Science and Whole Language Teacher Collaborative," continues to meet. They hope they can obtain new funding. They particularly want to establish an electronic mail system using LogoExpress. Telecommunications network would be used by students to share their ideas and projects.

### Emergence as Leaders

The MIT project brought publicity to the school. The joint meetings of the students in Reading and Lawrence brought media attention. Killam was visited by managers from the Lego Company's home office in Denmark. The entire staff at Killam is aware of the project through regular updates from the principal. The project has had an impact on all the fourth graders as Linda and Marty taught the other teachers to use *LegoLogo*. The fourth grade teachers could easily see the tie-in with the curriculum since they teach a unit on simple machines—perfect for *LegoLogo*. The first year of the project, Linda or Marty taught the lessons in *LegoLogo* while the classroom teacher assisted. The second year, the classroom teacher team-taught the lessons with either Linda or Marty. By year three, the other classroom teachers felt comfortable taking over the instruction.

## Obstacles to Using Technology

Both Linda and Marty report that there are obstacles to complete implementation of technology at their school. From paper to ribbons to software, money is short and requests are not always able to be filled. The computer equipment at the Killam is outdated and they do not foresee being able to purchase new equipment within the next few years. The school is receiving additional Apple IIe's as hand-me-downs from the high school. Marty and Linda would like to purchase a modem, a phone line, new computers, compact disc players, and laserdisc players.

In addition to equipment, Linda feels that many teachers at Killam would say that "time" is their biggest obstacle. It does take time to learn new programs and explore ways to use them in the curriculum. Even given the obstacles, Linda and Marty are generally pleased with the way technology is being used in their building. Approximately 90% of the teachers instruct with computers in an effective manner.

## School-wide Use of Technology

While the Logo project was going on, other efforts to improve the use of technology in the school were underway. The district continued to purchase computers (Apple IIe's). The librarian was instrumental in purchasing software. She spent a lot of time looking for quality software that fit in with the curriculum. She also worked with teachers to determine where to place the computers. The lab remained in the library and the rest of the computers were placed on carts so that they could be moved as necessary. Issues of scheduling the lab were worked out in an amicable fashion. Gradually more and more teachers started using the computers with their students. Many teachers took computer courses offered at the high school. The most popular courses were on *Appleworks* and on desktop publishing.

A district-wide curriculum revamping also spurred the implementation of technology. Every elementary teacher in the district is required to work on a curriculum committee. One committee formed was the "computer committee." The district identified computers as a target area for three years beginning with the 1990-91 school year. As part of the plan the district allocated funds to hire a computer consultant for the elementary grades. The part-time position would last for three years. Together the Assistant Superintendent and members of the computer committee interviewed a number of candidates for the consultant position. Marty had suggested a faculty member at Lesley College in the Computers in Education program. After the interviews, she was hired based on her philosophy, technical expertise, university connection, and background as an elementary teacher.

Working with the consultant, Linda, Marty, and the committee wrote a three-year plan and determined the ways to use the consultant's time (approximately

20 days per year). The plan emphasized the integration of computers into the curriculum and provided numerous opportunities for teachers to improve their expertise in teaching with computers. This extra commitment from the district helped what was already in motion at the Killam School. The central office purchased additional hardware and software. In 1990–91 The Killam School had 26 computers for their 570 students—a very modest number of computers. However, these computers were in constant use.

The computer committee decided to hold a series of workshops to allow teachers to brush up or learn new skills in a non-threatening environment. The workshops included topics such as early childhood software, word processing, tools for teachers, and Logo. The consultant conducted the workshops with the assistance of the computer committee members. Teachers could request that the consultant come to their classes and teach demonstration lessons. The computer committee rewrote the Logo curriculum for grades four and five emphasizing the integration into the curriculum.

### Advice for Improving Use of Technology

They offer the following advice to schools trying to integrate computers into the curriculum:

- Create a non-threatening environment where teachers feel comfortable exploring and making mistakes.
- Figure out ways to overcome teachers' fears, otherwise they will avoid technology.
- Show teachers how the software connects to the curriculum so they will not view it as yet another "add on" to an already crowded curriculum.
- Give teachers good access to equipment. Linda and Marty believe that having a lab as well as classroom computers on carts is ideal.
- Purchase appropriate software so teachers do not have to sift through lots of poor programs.
- Provide teachers with numerous chances for support—one-shot training will not work.

## Jonathan Choate

### Background

Jon graduated from Colby College in 1969, majoring in mathematics and sociology. He had wanted to become a pilot, but could not because of an automobile accident. Enjoying his work with children as a camp counselor, he chose a teaching career. Jon did his graduate work in mathematics, having found the one education course he tried not to his liking. His first job was teaching algebra and geometry in an independent school that specialized in students with reading problems. His next position was at the Groton School, where today he is the chair of the Mathematics Department. At Groton, Jon has taught everything from basic algebra to linear algebra and differential equations. He also teaches graduate education courses in integrating technology into the mathematics curriculum and simulation. He enjoys teaching people of all ages.

## First Encounter with Technology

Jon was not the first teacher in his school to use computers. Jon considers Roger Jarvis, the teacher who first used computers at Groton, as his mentor. Jon describes this teacher as a real visionary. Jon's mentor stayed at Groton for five years, until 1972. When he left, Jon carried on as the leader in bringing technology to his school. In 1967, Jon worked on a project with IBM and SRA to develop materials to integrate APL (A Programming Language) into the mathematics curriculum. This project resulted in his starting a computer program at Groton, using a Digital Equipment Company PDP computer, to integrate APL into the mathematics courses. Between the years 1972 and 1976 Jon, having lost interest in using computers to teach mathematics because he did not think the technology was going any place, experimented with audio-visual aids, especially videotapes. During these years he implemented a self-contained video-based mathematics course developed by Roger Jarvis.

In 1975 his interest in computers momentarily ignited again by a population simulation he saw on a Wang computer. However, the computer never went into production so a sustained interest did not develop. In 1980, he became intrigued by the potential of Apple's graphics capabilities to teach geometry. He also saw the computer's potential for word processing. At a local computer users' meeting, he heard a presentation of a simulation language called DYNAMO, the forerunner of STELLA, and the system dynamics approach to problem solving. Seeing many applications to secondary school mathematics, he and a colleague physics teacher began developing a new upper level mathematics curriculum around simulation. Through this curriculum they taught pre-calculus and calculus to the Groton students.

## Emergence as a Leader

Applied Mathematics, the upper level mathematics course initiated in 1980, is completely computer integrated. The course spans two years and students select it instead of advanced placement calculus. The course includes programming, system dynamics, differential calculus, probability and statistics, integral calculus, linear algebra, chaotic dynamical systems, and differential equations. The course ends with individual student projects applying the mathematics they have learned. Because of Jon's work developing the course, he was invited to be a co-author of the book, *Computers in Teaching Mathematics*.

Students apply various programming skills as soon as they learn them. In many cases, the students' programming is motivated by the problems they encounter; students develop programming skills in different languages as they need these skills to solve particular problems. As a result, students solve types of problems rarely found in high school mathematics courses.

### Obstacles to Using Technology

The universal obstacle to the spread of technology is teacher fear and ignorance. However, in inner-city schools in which Jon has worked, he has encountered obstacles that do not exist at Groton. With 45 students in a class there is very little access to equipment during school hours. As hand-held computers become a reality, this situation might be remedied.

### School-wide Use of Technology

The Groton administration has been extremely supportive of Jon's efforts. They give Jon free time to develop curriculum, to work outside of Groton on state-of-the-art software projects enabling him to keep abreast of the latest technologies, and provide funds from the school's endowment for necessary equipment. Some of Jon's recent projects include working with Robert Devaney at Boston University on material to integrate chaotic dynamical systems into the secondary mathematics curriculum and writing software for Houghton-Mifflin such as *Geometry Grapher* and *Fractal Factory*. Jon has worked to involve other teachers in using technology throughout his years at Groton. He continuously talks informally about the benefits of integrating technology; he demonstrates software whenever given the opportunity; he runs seminars whenever asked; and he shares all the materials he creates. Over the last five years, the ten mathematics teachers in his department all have integrated computers into their courses. Of the other 35 teachers at his school, 90% use word processing regularly, the science teachers use computers somewhat, the classics teacher uses a computer to create Latin materials, and the social studies teacher uses computers least. Jon predicts this will change as CD-ROMs become more available.

### Advice for Improving Use of Technology

From Jon's 25 years of experience he has learned that the most important element in spreading the use of technology is to make teachers comfortable with machines. He exposes them to the various technologies very slowly with a variety of demonstrations, then gives them plenty of time just to experiment. He finds today's technologies are so far ahead of the way teachers are thinking that teacher trainers must start wherever the teachers are. In addition, administrators and parents must also be educated every step along the way so that teachers receive the support they need for the effort required to integrate technology into their lives.

Jon believes that computers are just coming of age. Because of what machines make possible, they are actually shaping the mathematics curriculum and determining what can and should be taught. Computers have turned mathematics into an experimental science. The teacher's role is now that of an advisor and facilitator. However, because the College Boards are still a major determinant of student success, classes have not changed as dramatically as they should. College Boards force teachers to be content and outcome oriented rather than conduct class on a true experimental basis. However, the fact that, as of April, '93, ETS has allowed students to use graphing calculators while taking the mathematics achievement tests indicates society's changing views of technology.

Jon sees as some of the still unresolved issues:

- How much mathematics do people need to carry in their heads to be mathematics literate?
- Can we determine a body of mathematics that an educated citizen needs?
- How will access to technology be determined, both in and out of school?
- How will the tremendous teacher training needs be met—how will teachers keep up with advancing technologies?

Because the rate of change in the world is accelerating, people must understand how change affects the systems that effect their lives. Jon believes that simulations are an excellent tool for this purpose. His current objective is to help teachers get a handle on teaching about complex issues with the aid of dynamic simulations.

## Conclusions

The most important element to emerge from these interviews for sustaining leadership is support from other people. In all the cases documented here, the support came from both the school administration, generally the teacher's boss, and from some outside source. In Frank Draper's case a retired citizen seeking involvement in his new community and bringing with him a great deal of knowledge, skill, and comfort with technology is the key outside supporter. Gordon Brown, having spent the greater part of his life as an academic, is also quite sophisticated in the area of fund raising, which is an extremely important to the change movement now occurring in Frank's school district.

For Jon Choate the outside support comes from his continuing involvement in developmental software and curriculum projects. Again, because of the wisdom of his school administrators, he has been able to spend a meaningful amount of time on these projects even given the generally all-consuming life of a teacher at a boarding school. Work on these projects has not only kept Jon involved on the latest thinking in teaching mathematics with technology, but also has provided him with a support group of similarly minded colleagues.

For Linda Carey and Marty Pressey, outside support comes from their involvement with Seymour Papert at MIT. Papert's project not only introduced them to teaching with technology, but provided them with an ongoing support group of teachers.

Janis Rennie's outside support came from her association with Lesley College. Her initial relationship was as a part-time graduate student in the Computers in Education master's degree program. Following soon after graduation, Janis was asked to teach some of the courses in the program and has been an adjunct faculty since then. Coming on campus once a week or more to prepare for and teach her courses, she has constant access to Lesley's large software and hardware collections. In addition Janis works collaboratively with the full-time faculty of the program. This has created for her a support group of colleagues who share her interests and philosophy relating to technology in the schools.

Each of the interviewees has been fortunate to have strong in-school support. In the one instance, Chelsea, where the administration completely changed after Boston University's takeover, the teacher has chosen to leave the city for a job elsewhere. One of the important in-school features was the agreement by all the involved administrators to the goal of creating true interdisciplinary studies, something that the use of technology in education highlights and facilitates. This belief ties into a recommendation of all those interviewed: make sure technology augments the curriculum rather than making technology an "add on." It is interesting that the rest of the advice offered by these teachers is very similar even though, except for Marty and Linda, they do not know each other.

Given their very different education and expertise, in general, all the teachers made the following recommendations for educators working to integrate technology into their schools:

- Eliminate fear of machines. One technique is to make sure the teacher-trainer does not intimidate the students.
- Provide ongoing technical support in terms of local experts to answer immediate "how do I" inquiries, as well as continuous education on new versions of both software and hardware.
- Educate other school-interested people, such as parents and school boards, so they understand the time and effort it takes the teachers to stay current with respect to technology.

This is not new or remarkably insightful advice. These issues have been understood since the arrival of desktop computers. What is remarkable is that they still need to be said, that schools are still doing things, like offering one-day workshops, that do not work. Perhaps this is another instance of what Cuban (1992) identifies as a dilemma:

> In a can-do culture, a pervasive sense of guilt often haunts practitioners, professors, and policymakers who face recurring, insoluble situations and repeatedly fail to "solve" the "problem." Repeated failures of highly touted solutions leave a debris of disappointment, even cynicism, among well-intentioned educators. To distinguish between problems that can be solved and dilemmas that require "satisficing" can reduce guilt. We can pursue ways of reframing those dilemmas to get unstuck from familiar "solutions" and create better compromises or more elegant tightrope walks. (pp. 7–8)

It is time for teachers and administrators to get unstuck and get on with integrating technology into their schools.

## References

Cuban, L. (1992, Jan.–Feb.). Managing dilemmas while building professional communities. *Educational Researcher, 21*(1), 4–11.

Draper, F. (1989, May 2). Letter to Jay Forrester.

Draper, F. & Swanson, M. (1990, Summer). Learner-directed systems education: A successful example. *Systems Dynamics Review, 6*(2), 209–213.

Hopkins, P. L. (1991). *Simulating Hamlet in the Classroom.* Desert View High School, Tucson, AZ.

Kelman, P., Bardige, A., Choate, J., Hanify, G., Richards, J., Roberts, N., Walters, J. & Tornrose, M. K. (1983). *Computers in Teaching Mathematics.* Reading, MA: Addison-Wesley.

Meadows, D. *Fish Banks Simulation.* (n.d.). Creative Learning Exchange, 1 Keefe Rd., Acton, MA 01720.

Papert, S. (1980). *Mindstorms: Children, Computers, and Powerful Ideas.* New York: Basic Books.

Roberts, N., Andersen, D., Deal, R., Garet, M. & Shaffer, W. (1983). *Introduction to Computer Simulation: A System Dynamics Modeling Approach.* Reading, MA: Addison-Wesley.

Senge, P. (1990). *The Fifth Discipline. The Art and Practice of the Learning Organization.* New York: Doubleday.

## About the Authors

*Angeline Ferris* is an Assistant Professor at Lesley College and teaches in the Computers in Education program. In addition to her teaching at Lesley, she conducts workshops on integrating computers into the curriculum and works as a computer consultant in a local school system. She also co-developed and taught "Local History," a distance learning course for teachers. She received her Ed.M. from Temple University.

*Nancy Roberts* is currently Professor and Director of the Graduate Program in Computers in Education at Lesley College. Dr. Roberts has written a number of books about educational computing, serves as the editor of Prentice-Hall's Computers in Education Series, is on the Editorial Board of the *Journal of Educational Computing Research*, and is Vice Chair of the National Educational Computing Conference. She received her Ed.D. degree from Boston University.

# 6/ Turning Your Vision into Reality: SeniorNet and Apple Core

## Mary Furlong

University of San Francisco

## Martha Rolley

Apple Computer Inc.

*This chapter explores two visions of technology use which we have tried to implement in education on a national level—one involves older adults (age 55–95) and the other involves private school administrators and teachers. These two case studies describe how the germ of an idea can grow into a national program. We also discuss the steps to follow in expanding a vision. These include: clarifying an idea, identifying a champion and supporters, building a working team, identifying resources within your community and beyond, and finding the funding necessary to grow your vision.*

What is your vision for education? What role do you want to take as an educational leader in making your vision happen? How will your vision have an impact on the lives of many? These are questions that we ask of our graduate students. What we have discovered is that they usually do not think of themselves as visionary leaders—but rather as administrators and teachers. We first need to expand their awareness of their role as leaders and what they can accomplish. Our next task is to provide them with models of visionary educational programs—at the national, state, and local school levels. Finally, we need to share ideas about the steps they might take in making their vision become a reality.

These steps also involve a "revisioning" of the original ideas and a plan to take your vision to the next level. Within this process, we always continue to grow as leaders—mastering new skills in management, resource gathering, and communication of our results.

## SeniorNet: The Initial Vision

SeniorNet had its origins in an informal project that began in the summer of 1983 by Mary Furlong and Greg Kearsley. We observed that a large component of the population (i.e., people over 60) were not getting any attention from the computer world. This raised a number of questions in our minds: Were senior citizens interested in computers? In what kinds of programs would they be interested? Did they have special needs in terms of hardware or software?

To satisfy our curiosity, we began to give computer workshops in church basements and senior citizen centers using inexpensive home computers with used TV sets as monitors. By the end of the summer we had taught hundreds of seniors to use computers. To make a long story short, we discovered that many older adults were *very* interested in computers, and that they had no particular problems learning to use them. This vision grew.

Somewhere along the way, a dream was born. The dream was to establish a telecommunications network to link together computer-using seniors. With help from many people and a few enlightened sponsors, this dream grew into SeniorNet.

## SeniorNet Today

SeniorNet is now a non-profit organization, based in San Francisco, with over 5,000 members whose mission is to provide older adults with access to computer technologies and, thereby, enable them to share their wisdom and talents with the rest of society. The organization operates SeniorNet Online, a telecommunications network for older adults. SeniorNet offers computer instruction at more than 40 local Learning Centers throughout the United States and in New Zealand (see Figure 1) and provides instructional materials to its members who may not be located near a center. It also holds a biannual conference for computer-using seniors.

Staff members administer the network, provide training and support for the Learning Centers, create informational and instructional products for the members, enroll new members, organize the conference, and conduct research on the use of computers by older adults. SeniorNet has received financial support from many organizations, including the John and Mary R. Markle Foundation, Apple Computer, Inc., IBM, the Pacific Telesis Foundation, Pacific Bell, the Bell Atlantic Foundation, the Goldsmith Foundation, American Express, and U S West.

Figure 1. SeniorNet Learning Centers.

## SeniorNet Learning Centers

SeniorNet helps individuals and organizations who want to establish local SeniorNet Learning Centers for computer instruction. Learning Centers are places where seniors come to learn about and use computers. SeniorNet Learning Centers are located in such diverse locations as senior centers, schools and universities, eye clinics, and hospitals.

At each Learning Center there are classes designed to introduce seniors to computer applications. The SeniorNet curriculum, *SeniorWorks*, based on *Microsoft Works*, includes courses such as: "Introduction to Computers," "Wordprocessing," "SpreadSheets," and "Databases." Typically, classes are offered for 1–2 hours once a week for six to eight weeks. Classes are small in size (about 10 participants) and the instruction is "hands on" with the computer.

The introductory course is one of the most popular classes at each SeniorNet Learning Center.

At each Learning Center, there is "open lab time" for members to practice their skills. During this time, members may also use the computers to create materials and flyers for their other activities. In our San Francisco and Las Vegas Learning Centers, for example, members publish a newsletter.

SeniorNet helps Learning Centers get started by providing assistance in locating a sponsor, organizing the center, and training the coordinator and computer instructors. To become a SeniorNet Learning Center, an organization needs a secure facility for equipment, a coordinator with good organizational skills, and a sponsor. Sponsors include businesses, foundations, and individuals who are willing to provide the financial support for Learning Centers. Sponsors also subsidize online network time for classes in which members learn to use the SeniorNet Online network.

## SeniorNet Online

SeniorNet operates an online telecommunications network that links participants in SeniorNet Learning Centers and individual members throughout the United States and Canada. It provides support for the Learning Centers and gives individual seniors with the means to communicate with one another and to gain access to information on a variety of subjects. The host network for SeniorNet Online is America Online (see Figure 2).

Any individual with a SeniorNet membership can establish an account and join the online network. To participate in SeniorNet Online, you need a computer, telecommunications software, and a modem to connect your computer with your phone line. In most cities and towns members are able to use a local telephone number to connect to the network, so there are no long distance charges. Members are billed monthly for their network use at a flat rate of $9.95 a month, which covers unlimited use of the network weekdays after 6 p.m. local time and all day Saturday and Sunday within the SeniorNet area. At other times, hourly rates apply.

Once you learn another member's user name, you can send electronic mail to the new friends you meet in the member directory. Electronic mail is private—so this is the place to send your love notes! Or, you can participate in a live conference where members gather together from their computers to discuss topics such as Medicare, genealogy, or who will win the Superbowl. Real-time conferences allow members to be online at the same time. However, most of the time, information and opinion are posted in the SeniorNet Forums. The Forums allow members to follow a topic of interest—such as health, politics, or retirement, but it is not done in real time. Instead, you express your opinion and then others read and respond to it whenever they have time to sign on to their

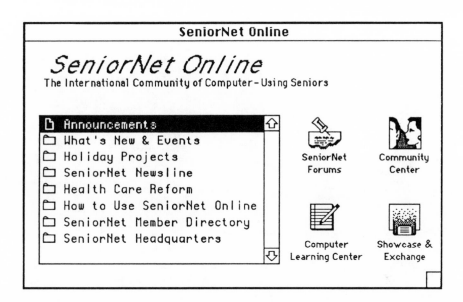

Figure 2. Main Menu for SeniorNet Online.

computers. The Forum allows one to read the comments made by various members.

Here is a sample listing of the SeniorNet Forum's folders (the number indicates the total messages in that forum):

| | |
|---|---|
| Abortion Rights | 329 |
| "Almost Oval Office" | 197 |
| Announcements | 259 |
| Arts & Entertainment | 248 |
| Battle of...??! | 418 |
| Economics | 170 |
| Food, Drink, & Recipes | 156 |
| Freethinkers Forum | 450 |
| Gardening | 450 |
| Gay & Lesbian Senior Issues | 125 |
| Gun Control | 282 |
| The Hearth | 450 |
| Introductions | 450 |
| Jewish Interests | 147 |

| | |
|---|---|
| Jokes & Clever Quips | 390 |
| Learning | 433 |
| Men's Forum | 381 |
| Newcomer's / Lurker's Forum | 271 |
| Person-to-Person | 450 |
| Pets | 118 |
| Poetry/Limericks | 307 |
| Politics | 450 |
| Sex!! | 190 |
| Travel | 203 |
| Where in the world is???? | 190 |
| Women's Forum | 201 |
| Writing | 297 |

SeniorNet members have debated various issues in the Forum. Often, the network serves as an interactive diary—allowing people to record their thoughts and feelings when they wish to share them with other members. For example, here is a message from the General Forum left by Joan Elswitt, SeniorNet member from Warrenton, Virginia.

> *What I am talking about when I say 'dustbowl,' Roosevelt, NRA, the years of the godforsaken Okies. SeniorNet has given me a place to talk with people my own age...I can't travel as much as I once did, but with SeniorNet I roam the United States with great joy.*

The network also offers special forums created by members. One popular meeting place for beginners as well as advanced users is the "Getting into Computers Forum." It is here that members can ask questions about their specific hardware and software configurations.

Through SeniorNet Online, it is possible for seniors to communicate with their grandchildren. SeniorNet members enter the network through SeniorNet and their grandchildren through the regular America Online service. As one SeniorNet member said, "I am buying them a modem for their computer and instead of writing letters once in a great while, I will go online with them maybe two or three times a week. I can't think of anything that will make me happier." Alan Kay of Apple Computer describes this as the "extended family," connected electronically.

In the SeniorNet Online Forum, "Generation to Generation," SeniorNet members participate in organized intergenerational activities. In this area school children communicate with older adults on a wide variety of topics. One example is the continuing correspondence of SeniorNet members with young people from Mesa Verde High School, near Sacramento:

*Subj: Mesa Verde High School Arrives!*      *91-12-04 19:05:15 EDT*

*From: SeniorNet*

*Posted on: America Online*

*We are students at Meda Verde High School. We are located at 7600 Lauppe Lane, Citrus Heights, CA, 95621. The land was donated by Sharon Van Maren. The School opened in 1974. The land that this school is sitting on was farmland. Meda Verde was never completed because of Prop 13. The district stopped building because of lack of money. Before Mesa Verde started, the district was rich. Then after that started to go downhill from then on. We have 4 of the teachers who have been here since they opened. They are Mr. Sears, Mr. Paulat, Mr. Anderson, Ms. Taylor. Mr. Sears is the library teacher. Mr. Paulat is the art teacher. Ms. Taylor is the aerobics teacher. Mr. Anderson is the wood shop teacher. Our school is 88.4% white, 2.3% black, 5.7% hispanic, .9% philipino, 2% islander, .8% alaskan native. This was our survey on January 15, 1991. Mesa Verde is built on 38.3 acres and it has 46 classrooms. Why we are called Mavericks? It is because of a guy in the 1870's who owned a herd of cattle in a poker game. He never branded his cattle and let them run free. Maverick came to mean someone who goes against tradition and does a thing his or her own way. And we the students are looking forward to talking to you.*

---

*Subj: Mindee Brown*      *92-09-30 22:02:49 EST*

*From: ENID FLA*

*Posted on: America Online*

*Hi, I'm from Fla (didn't get the hurricane) and I thought you might like to correspond with me because I am an EMT. I have been one for 8 years. I am 72 yrs old and I work every eighth day for 24 hours at a time. Before I retired, I was a high school teacher and taught math and computers. I also coached their coed swimming team. You can leave messages here for me.*

---

*Subj: to Enid FL*                          *92-10-07 16:41:47 EST*

*From: SR 2 Sr*

*Posted on: America Online*

*Hi Enid Fla,*

*Could you tell me somethings you saw while you were working in the EMT. I like to go swimming and played softball and any kind of sport. I have a great great great aunt who is 101 years old and she is still going strong. What course did you take before you become an EMT and how long did it take to become an EMT. So I will know how long the schooling takes before I become an EMT.*

*Mindee Brown*

*Mesa Verde High School*

## Other SeniorNet Activities

SeniorNet develops informational and instructional materials for its members. These products range from pamphlets on how to buy a computer to software templates on how to manage personal finances or inventory a coin collection. SeniorNet provides materials in a variety of formats: written pamphlets and electronic files for several types of computers. SeniorNet members are often involved in the creation of these products for other members.

Every other year, SeniorNet holds a national conference for computer-using seniors. The conference includes presentations, hands-on workshops, and exhibits. Sessions are given by experts on many computer-related topics. SeniorNet members also present new ideas. The conferences give SeniorNet members an opportunity to meet one another and exchange ideas. They also provide a chance for learning center coordinators to obtain more training and share their experiences. In June 1992, the focus of the Fourth Conference was a "SeniorFest," highlighting the activities and sharing the materials created by our SeniorNet community. This SeniorFest was presented on Capitol Hill where representatives of 40 Congressional Offices observed the projects created by SeniorNet members.

## Apple Core: The Initial Vision

In 1984 the second author was principal of a K–8 elementary school (St. Mark School in Venice, California). I was just about to finish my Master's degree in Private School Administration at the University of San Francisco. That spring, however, conscience, guilt, and a class taught by Mary Furlong on the uses of technology in curriculum conspired to change my life.

I didn't need any more classes or units but I was nagged by the realization that I hadn't taken any courses about computer technology and I felt a little insecure about finishing my degree work without even engaging in a token survey of this computer phenomena that seemed to be getting increasing attention in educational journals. Thus, when the University of San Francisco offered a course in instructional uses of computers, I decided to assuage my guilt and take it for two units. Three units required a project. I didn't think I needed to do a project—I was only interested in a survey of the situation from the theoretical position of a principal. I was destined to be very surprised because from the first class with Mary Furlong, I was drawn into a new world of possibilities that elicited from me spontaneous, enthusiastic, and genuine participation.

Like all principals, I was always looking for ways to improve office efficiency and increase my professionalism. During the class with Mary, I began to extend my explorations into programs that could impact the school office. I started to explore the potential of the Apple IIe and the *VisiCalc* spreadsheet to transform the way that I did my annual budget preparation and was impressed with the results. The process offered great improvements in accuracy and the magical ability to experiment with critical factors and instantly see the bottom-line results.

One of the reasons that I was personally compulsed into taking this course about computers was that it seemed to me the entire rest of the world was already utilizing technology and I believed that I was woefully behind in my profession. Timidly, I mentioned my budget project to my neighboring principals, and to my great surprise, I discovered that they were no farther along in implementing technology into their offices and were generally beginners or "wanna-bees" along with me. Thus, with confidence born of peer support, I continued to develop the budget template and a tutorial on how to use the Apple IIe called "Apple Ease." These I offered to principals in workshops and found an enthusiastic audience and a great interest in continuing this type of inservice training. Since the Archdiocese of Los Angeles did not have technology training centers or support personnel for technology, efforts in this area had to be managed on an individual or grass roots level.

In the meantime, I had completed my MA and the course with Mary Furlong, but not before she had approached me and spoken the unthinkable ... would I consider going on into the doctoral program? I tried to explain that she was addressing the great procrastinator and the epitome of the non-eternal student— the person who had taken her course for two instead of three units. I was, however, in a bad position to argue. Not only is Mary hard to dissuade once she is in her "enthusiasm" mode, but I had been bitten for the first time in my life with a internally driven desire to learn more. I wanted to learn more about computers and I had discovered that I enjoyed teaching others what I had learned. I had caught Mary's enthusiasm and I could not get rid of it. Despite the fact that I had a mental disjoint with the vision of me in a doctoral program (how soon would it be before they discovered how truly untalented I was?), I applied to the University of San Francisco. By some miracle, they accepted me into the doctoral program in Private School Administration with an emphasis in Educational Technology.

As I took my doctoral classes and continued to serve as principal and conduct periodic "Apple Ease" computer workshops, I began to dream of the time when there would be widespread inservice training in the Archdiocese of Los Angeles that would be supported by a partnership between Apple Computer, Inc., and Archdiocesan personnel. A number of circumstances came together that caused a plan to form that would accomplish this dream. First, in one of my classes I was assigned to do program design on a Macintosh. I didn't have a Macintosh. I only had Apple II computers. Second, and with fortuitous timing, Apple invited me to participate in their "Test Drive a Macintosh" promotion. I was instantly enthralled with the ease of use and the power that the Macintosh offered. I saw it as the perfect tool for the administrator because its intuitive interface made it low on the techie scale but high on productivity. It was the perfect "Apple Ease" and I began to work on plans to convert my school office from Apple to Macintosh and to translate all our files from *AppleWorks* into *Microsoft Works*.

Gradually, plans came together in my mind to form a group of volunteers who would serve as trainers for schools who wished to learn more about how they could use software with their curriculums. I mapped out the program in detail, including the need for some loaner computers from Apple Computer, and called it "Apple Core." Before approaching Apple with the proposal, I secured permission from the Superintendent of the Archdiocese to represent them in discussions with Apple. Thus, armed with permission and proposal, I met with the Apple Account Executive for the Archdiocese. To my surprise, I received a very open response and a willingness to explore the possibility of supporting the "Apple Core" program. After further discussions and some refinements of the program, Apple agreed to provide loaner equipment for demonstration schools and to support the "train the trainer" concept of Apple Core. We were on our way!

## Apple Core: The Vision Grows

A handful of interested volunteers began to meet once a month at my school to be trained on basic computing operations and specific software that companies donated or loaned to our software library. We loaned software to individuals and schools for review, and the Apple Core Trainers conducted inservice workshops for faculties. Five schools in the Archdiocese received

Apple IIc computers and were designated as "demonstration" schools. Inservices were conducted at these schools, and other school faculties visited them to see how they were implementing the technology into their curriculum.

From this beginning group of Apple Core Trainers, the Archdiocesan Elementary Computing Consortium (AECC) was born and in time became a broad based technology resource for the entire Archdiocese. As time progressed, it became increasingly apparent to me that a critical first step in getting technology integrated into the classroom was to help administrators become users of it. I believed that if administrators could have a personal experience of the power of technology in their daily office operations, then they would become actively interested in advancing it into their classrooms. I reflected on my own personal story and realized that it wasn't until I began to actually use computers myself that I gave discussion and budget priority to educational technology. Before that time it was just a "fringe" issue or a "frill." My perspective had changed to seeing technology not as a frill but rather as an essential of life for educational management, student productivity, and curriculum delivery.

Thus, the concept of "Apple Core" became focused on providing administrators and then teachers with the skills that they needed to integrate technology tools into their professions. I was able to teach summer courses on administrative uses of computers at the University of San Francisco and started to refine the Apple Core materials to address administrative training and educational management skills.

In time, I completed my doctoral work and a year later was informed that my 13 years at St. Mark School would soon come to an end as I was to be transferred to another principalship. Coincidentally, Apple Computer was restructuring. Much to my surprise, they asked me if I would consider coming to work in the K–12 education group in their newly formed western operational headquarters with responsibility for private schools. It was an exciting opportunity to pursue my dream of sharing technology with educators on an even wider scale, and I accepted.

I expanded the Apple Core vision further to seeing schools across the nation linked electronically. A company called CONNECT™ brought that vision to reality by providing a low cost and customizable electronic communication program. Today there are thousands of schools across the United States that are able to send electronic mail and share educational resources as well as ideas instantly. I believed then as I do now that electronic mail has the power to be a great leadership tool.

Superintendents from California to New York have transformed the way that they do business with each other and their schools because of their openness to learning about technology and what it could offer for their systems. Through their leadership, schools are linked electronically and receive weekly if not daily communication from the central office as well as other schools. Contents of messages can range from information about upcoming workshops, to reminders about deadlines, to requests for assistance or offers to share surplus materials. Turn-around time on information has become a matter of hours instead of days and weeks. Documents and forms are also transmitted via electronic mail, making obsolete large printings and storage. Now printing is done as needed at the school site.

The best comment that I have heard relative to the transformational power of electronic communication came from a superintendent who stood up and admitted to her peers that she was concerned about getting into technology and especially e-mail because she feared that it would depersonalize and dehumanize the participants. To her great surprise, she found that it accomplished the exact opposite. Principals were much more communicative and supportive of each other with electronic mail than they were with the U. S. Postal Service and telephone. She reported that social events happened more frequently and spontaneously via electronic mail than before when telephone tag or long lead times for mail took too much energy. Now one memo can be written and sent instantly to multiple recipients with no muss–no fuss and the assurance that it will be read in the next 24 hours—if not sooner.

I have become the corporate director of private schools for Apple Computer and am still motivated daily by the desire to contribute to the development of an information age educational system. Through the years, I have been sustained and energized by my association with tremendously talented and generous co-workers at Apple as well as dedicated educators who have participated in the Apple Core program. The shared vision of a new model of education that exists among these people is exciting and challenging. One of the projects that I have collaborated in at Apple to communicate this vision is an interactive tool designed to assist K–12 educators in planning for education in the 21st century called *Teaching, Learning, & Technology—A Planning Guide*. It is especially intended to help integrate education planning with technology planning, and to show the value of technology to overall curriculum and instructional objectives. I have learned a great deal in the process of working on this project with others at Apple.

## Apple Core: Reflecting on the Vision

Over time, there have been, of course, high and hopeful moments such as when a superintendent adopts the vision of technology integrated into education and successfully implements the Apple Core program. There have also been the difficult and down times when leaders seem apathetic or unwilling to take bold, decisive action in order to achieve organizational growth. My greatest joy is seeing educational leaders seize the vision and the opportunity to move their organizations ahead from the top down. They give their principals courage and they actively participate in what they request. My greatest frustration is to see organizations with grass root energies unable to come together as a strong whole for lack of leadership that is willing to set timelines and objectives for fear of resistance and negative feedback from some. At these times I wonder about the efficacy of everything—including myself.

The challenges and stresses that exert themselves most in my life are around how to communicate the vision of a new educational culture to those who don't want to see it or work toward change and, second, how to assist others in acquiring the technological skills that are so necessary to accomplish this educational transformation. The enormity of the needed change sometimes is overwhelming and it is easy to get caught up in the small daily impediments that strain to make one cry out "I can't." The most important statements that I try to communicate are "we can do it together" and "we can't afford not to try."

The vision that Mary Furlong passed on to me has become my passion. My work at Apple allows me to meet and evangelize many people with this vision of a new educational culture. I have been able to develop the Apple Core model into a "train the trainer" program that is available to all private school organizations in the United States. Both my position at Apple Computer as well as my adjunct professorship at the University of San Francisco have allowed me to pursue my original dream for inservice training in creative ways that were beyond my wildest hopes.

In the beginning a spark of leadership was kindled in me. My original vision was to transform my own productivity and my school. Gradually that expanded to include hopes for the schools locally in the Archdiocese of Los Angeles. Now, that vision and dream have grown and is being realized nationally as certified Apple Core trainers reside in all the regions of the United States.

## A Model for Making Your Vision Happen

Based upon our experiences in these two case studies, we offer the following four-stage model to making a vision happen.

### 1. Discovering the Vision Within You

Both of these case studies describe a process involving three critical elements: the learners (children in school, teachers and administrators, and older adults), the curriculum—training both formal and informal, and the society these learners are about to enter. We have tried to construct new paradigms for how learners are prepared to live in their changing technological world.

Our quest was to seek new ways of teaching and learning that would enhance the lives of our students. Mary Furlong's vision related to restoring the role of older adults as leaders in our society. She knew that many older people were retired from occupations as teachers, scientists, doctors, and librarians. For these people, playing "golf" was not going to be enough. They were lifelong learners and there were few programs available to support their needs and interests. They had limited access to computers in the workplace and they did not exist when most older people were in school. So her vision was shaped around providing older adults with access to technology to enhance their lives and the lives of others. Telecommunications would be able to allow them to share their ideas with one another and to provide a means to access information.

Martha Rolley cared passionately about improving the world of private education. She understood the role of private school principals as educational leaders. She had an insight as to how a network could help support their needs for communication and collaboration. She also knew the critical independent role that private school administrators had in being able to effect change within their own school communities.

Technology became a tool to support this learning process. The vision for SeniorNet and Apple Core came from within our imaginations and was greatly improved by the discussion of "what if?" with thousands of others. So, the first step is to *imagine* yourself as an educational leader. Consider your work in the past. Did it call for collaborative learning, curriculum integration, use of outside resources? What role can technology play in this vision?

## 2. Finding Champions and Supporters

In both of our endeavors, the dreams existed in some small way at the start. When Greg and Mary created SeniorNet, they did it with home computers purchased from the toy store and rented television sets. They looked for funding for two years before they found the Markle Foundation in 1983. This was a very difficult time; most visions fail at this point. People do not pursue their ideas to the fullest; they stop before they find the investors who can make them grow. Often, they get discouraged. A dream takes a champion to make it happen. You need a few people who believe in it and will stay with you until you find your first investor.

Your team can be quite diverse. It may include teachers, other administrators, parents, students, and volunteers. At Pescadero High School, the computer coordinator has a wonderful project in which science education has become a central focus of the school. This teacher has enlisted support and involvement of the entire community, from a local documentary filmmaker to the janitor of the school. When you create the team, be sure to have total "buy in" to your vision and then think creatively about the possible players. We have had over 500 volunteers who essentially run our SeniorNet program at the Learning Centers. Most of these volunteers did not have careers in the field of education. Yet, they are dedicating more than ten hours a week to teaching! They have been the real ones who make the dream happen!

### 3. Acquiring Resources

When you begin a project, you must be very creative in finding resources within your community and beyond. Resources may take the form of time that volunteers have to spend on a project. Or, they may take the form of contributed equipment, supplies, or other expertise. As educators in private schools for many years, Martha and Mary learned that you could "make do" with 85% of the budget. We became skilled at bartering. In SeniorNet, for example, we have an advertising agency that contributes pro bono time and a public relations agency that also provides help on a pro bono basis.

Parents in the school community are a great place to begin. After all, who has more of a vested interest in the results of the programs. Many older adults have expertise and a desire to contribute. The role of the leader is to identify these potential resources and share the vision with them. The next step is to clearly communicate how they can be of service in implementing your programs. Finally, you must keep them "in the loop" and provide them with opportunities to shape the program further. Also, you should seek ways to give them recognition for their contribution.

### 4. Finding the Funding

To help an idea grow—like Apple Core or SeniorNet—you must have other sponsors that shape and support it. Martha was fortunate to go to Apple and have them provide the resources to help her program grow on a national level. We were fortunate to find the Markle Foundation and Apple Computer in 1986. Markle provided the "social venture capital" that allowed the vision of SeniorNet to grow and reach many people.

When you want to find additional support for your vision, you need to be able to communicate your ideas clearly—both orally and in writing. You will be asked to write a one or two page summary of your vision. This letter must state your purpose, your audience, your methods, and the intended outcomes. These outcomes will need to match with the goals of a funding agency.

If you are successful in getting a funding agency to read your letter, you should be prepared to write a longer proposal explaining the idea further and including a budget. Circulate drafts of your plan to critical reviewers before you send it to a funding agency.

Pursue your vision. Dreams only happen when you share them. There really is nothing more rewarding than watching your small dream grow into a wonderful reality.

## About the Authors

*Mary Furlong* is a Professor of Education at the University of San Francisco and President of SeniorNet, Inc. She has written a number of articles on educational computing and created several award-winning curriculum packages. She was a high school social sciences teacher for seven years and received her Ed.D. from the University of Southern California in 1979.

*Martha Rolley* is the director of private school marketing at Apple Computer, Inc. Dr. Rolley was an elementary school teacher and principal for many years before joining Apple. She received her Ed.D. in private school administration from the University of San Francisco in 1989.

# 7/ Designing the Future: The Florida Schoolyear 2000 Initiative

## Robert K. Branson & Atsusi Hirumi

**Florida State University**

*This chapter examines the process of designing an alternative system of public education that will compete with other emerging models and enable youth to succeed in a global, information-based society. The leadership implications for the new system are presented in context of various system features and are summarized at the conclusion of the chapter. A brief history of the Florida Schoolyear 2000 Initiative and a description of its components is combined with the research basis for adopting or including specific features. A description of the political and social context of education in the 1980s begins the chapter.*

## The Context

Numerous commissions, politicians, and concerned citizens advocate a plethora of solutions to the educational problems in the United States. These solutions range from relatively simple, one variable fixes to the most profound approaches to educational reform ever offered. In *A Nation At Risk* (National Commission on Excellence in Education, 1983), recommendations predominated to expand the current system, including lengthening the school day and year. Other experts and politicians recommend changes, ranging from fine-tuning existing practices (e.g., making student evaluation more authentic), to the complete dissolution of the current system, replacing it with vouchers and choice programs intended to create an educational free market (Lemann, 1991; Chubb & Moe, 1990; Gwartney, 1990; Firestone, Fuhrman & Kirst, 1989).

More than 95% of educators we have questioned are, predictably, opposed to voucher and choice programs. Yet, there was intense pressure from the Bush administration to eliminate the educational bureaucracy (Bush, 1992). We believe that public educators must respond by building and installing more competitive educational systems; the social climate of the times will not sustain business as usual. The collapse of the Soviet Union provides vivid evidence that huge central government organizations can be dismantled; ideas of this kind quickly spread to other institutions (see Shanker, 1988).

Many of the proposed solutions focus on adjusting, repairing, or stimulating the current educational system. Higher standards for teachers and students, increased funding, longer school days, and greater effort are supposed to increase school productivity. An alternative interpretation of the data suggests, however, that the problems in education are caused by obsolete operational processes, not faulty people or low standards (Branson, 1988).

The majority of change advocates presuppose the traditional teacher-student model as inviolable; they assume that the existing paradigm is sufficient to meet current and future demands. We argue that the current school model is obsolete. That is, it reached the upper limit of its potential effectiveness and efficiency many years ago. Reasoning by analogy, we conclude that the traditional fixes offered to public education would be similar to claiming that if the executives and crews at American Airlines worked longer and harder, they could use existing aircraft to take a man to the moon and return him safely to earth. We reject the notion that more effort or more money applied *within the context of the existing school model* would produce significant and lasting improvements.

Figure 1 represents the generic maturity curve of technologies through time; it applies well to numerous fields of endeavor (see Smith, 1981). As with most technologies, education began with a period of slow development, went through a period of rapidly increasing productivity, and has now approached the upper limit of its design capabilities. Dial telephones, railroad telegraphs, steam locomotives, and 300-baud modems represent instances of technologies that long ago reached their maximum performance.

We believe that the teachers, principals, and students are working about as hard as they can. Urging them to work harder, within the current operational model, will yield variable and insignificant improvements. These conclusions were supported when, in both the 1970s and 1980s, the real cost of education increased by 50% (Perelman, 1990). A resource increase of 50% in any system should yield an impressive increase in results or outcomes. When no improvements occurred, that provided additional evidence of obsolescence. We believe that no amount of additional funds or effort will result in substantial and lasting improvements to the current operations model.

The introduction of new technologies in public schools further illustrates the need for systemic change. Beginning in the 1970s, numerous papers have dealt with the use of microcomputers and other media. Computers were simply overlaid on the existing classroom organization. Subsequently, as experience

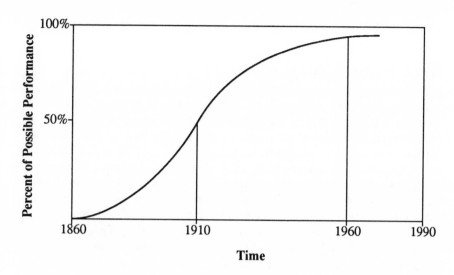

Figure 1. The Maturity of a Technology Through Time (after C. S. Smith, 1981).

accumulated, numerous articles questioned the value of computers for education. Traditionalists were relieved. To them, the technology had failed. However, even a cursory analysis of the processes used to implement computers could have predicted the lack of significant improvements; computers were simply added to existing processes, and frequently modeled the ineffective procedures already in place.

Conversely, the implementation of computer technologies and optical character recognition devices in other sectors of the society made huge improvements in outcomes and service availability. It became evident that there is a profound difference between using technology effectively and adding technology to an existing structure. There is a fundamental law that applies to the application of technology to any operational process: technology does not reduce costs or improve results; managers do.

Next, we describe the design and development of Florida's Schoolyear 2000 (SY2000) Initiative; one approach to creating a new system of education. We begin with background information about the initiative, including a description of its mission, approach, and design principles. A new paradigm for education is then introduced, followed by a description of the SY2000 operations model and key system processes (see Branson, 1990). We proceed to discuss the concurrent design, consensus building, and co-development processes that were used to create the SY2000 model. We conclude this chapter by summarizing the implications for educational technology leadership.

## The Schoolyear 2000 Initiative

The State of Florida has about 2.3 million students and about 120,000 teachers with an annual budget of approximately $9.8 billion. The Florida population is highly diverse, incorporating some 55 language groups across a geographical expanse of 800 miles from Pensacola to Key West. Northern communities are principally agricultural and military, and southern communities are mostly urban with agriculture, international trade, and tourism making up large portions of the economy. Central Florida has been devoted to high technology industry and the space program, with dramatic increases in tourism since the opening of Disney World in 1971.

In the mid-1980s, staff at the Center for Educational Technology (CET) at Florida State University began an analysis and design process intended to yield an alternative model of schooling for the state of Florida. In 1989, the Florida Department of Education (DOE) asked CET to direct a multi-year initiative to design and implement technology-based models of schooling that would be capable of producing results significantly better than those possible within the context and constraints of the current educational system. We reasoned that if other successful sectors of the society depended on technology to improve performance, education could learn from those successes. During 1990, the SY2000 focused on the planning activities and data collection necessary to prepare for a major initiative. The Initiative has now entered the design and development phase, which began with definition of a mission and approach.

### SY2000 Approach

The SY2000 Initiative will implement technology-based models that will enable students to use creative learning and research tools to become independent learners. This model will use design principles derived from modern research in learning, motivation, instructional design, and knowledge organization and engineering. A quality system that meets international quality standards will guide the total schooling process. The mission statement is: "All children will acquire the profound knowledge they need to succeed in adult life assessments."

### Design Principles

To direct the design and development work of the SY2000 Initiative, the design principles in Table 1 were developed and adopted by the DOE, CET and collaborating school districts.

## Table 1.
## Schoolyear 2000 Design Principles.

| Design Principle | Description |
|---|---|
| Learner Centered | The new model supports individual learning and involves learners in directing and evaluating their own learning and progress. Learners participate in selecting their learning tasks. Learners work in settings best suited for the attainment of the specific learning tasks. |
| Systems Approach | A set of interrelated functions acting together to accomplish a predetermined purpose where information about the system is used in an interative process to continually increase its effectiveness and efficiency. |
| Quality System | A quality system that meets the ANSI/ASQC Q90-Q94 standards (ISO 9000-9004) will be used to assure the sound application of quality science theory and practice to schooling. |
| Technology Based | The new model will apply scientific knowledge to all aspects of the learning process and to management, support services, staff development and other functions of education. |
| Incrementally Improvable | A mechanism for making regular improvements and assuring that those improvements remain through time. The model is organized into segments so that alternative approaches can be readily interchanged. |
| Affordable | After initial start-up expenditures, operational costs will increase more slowly and level off when the model is fully operational. Reallocation of existing resources should allow for maintenance. |
| Learner Contribution | Processes that allow learners to contribute their knowledge and skills to system operations, e.g., peer tutoring, community service, on campus work. |
| Concurrent Design | All of the functions of the new model will be designed concurrently. Those individuals and groups that will implement the new model will participate in suggesting performance requirements and coming to consensus on those requirements. |
| Replicable | Successful operation of the model should not be dependent on the presence of an extraordinary principal or teacher. Staff must be able to effectively operate the model. |
| Electronic Tools | In the new model the student will interact with adults, eletronic systems, and with other students. It is through this paradigm that students assume responsibility for their own learning. |
| Integrity of Implementation | All collaborating districts will test the entire model as designed. |

**New Paradigm**

Examination of successful operations models in other sectors of society, such as science, reveals that it is often new paradigms that cause major improvements to a system. As we move into the 21st century, two significant events have stimulated the need for shifting today's educational paradigm. First, both the amount of information and the desire to rapidly access that information have increased exponentially. Second, the capacity for technologies to store, access, and manipulate information has greatly expanded.

Figure 2 presents the traditional educational paradigm, where teachers provide instruction based on their own knowledge and experience. The teacher, in this paradigm, is the primary source of information, and controls the order of presentation. This method of information transfer from teachers to students cannot exceed 300 baud. That is, the information transfer process is limited by the limited speed of voice transmission.

It is known, however, that students have the capability to input considerably faster rates of information if they can access and control them. With 300 baud of voice transmission being the upper limit, it becomes evident that no major improvements in the knowledge transfer process will occur without a dramatic increase in data transmission rates.

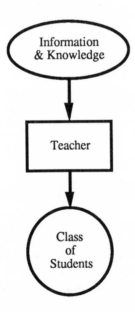

Figure 2. Traditional Educational Paradigm.

Figure 3 presents the revised paradigm of instruction for the Schoolyear 2000 Initiative. The paradigm contains several critical features. First, modern storage technologies enable us to provide access to the accumulated knowledge of humankind at a student workstation. Intelligent interfaces and electronic performance support systems (EPSS) also give students access to the combined knowledge of the best teachers. Thus, with an intelligent interface, a mixed initiative approach can be implemented in which the student can request assistance from the electronic "coach," or the coach can monitor the performance of the student and intervene at appropriate times. Giving students direct access to the database and a constant coaching capability to assist them in processing and using information provides a dramatic increase in the rate of knowledge transfer from the system to students (Gery, 1991). This critical shift has changed the technical upper limit of information transfer. Students can now access and manipulate information at faster rates as they become more proficient on the system. Students become proficient at accessing the information database through appropriate communications protocols, removing the limitation imposed on them by the old paradigm.

Another critical feature of the new paradigm is that it takes into account each student's accumulated knowledge and experience. Technology facilitates information delivery by giving learners a variety of options based on an ongoing

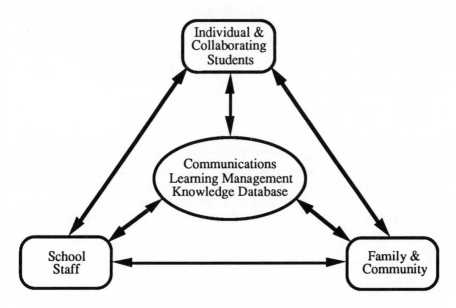

Figure 3. The Technology-Based Paradigm Used in the SY2000 Design.

assessment of each student's interests, motivation, and cognitive ability. It is through this paradigm that the major goal of preparing students to assume responsibility for their own learning is possible. By providing direct access to the knowledge-base, the new paradigm challenges students to manage and manipulate vast amounts of information while encouraging them to reflect on their own learning. It enables students to change roles from a passive recipient of information to an active knowledge worker. It is the intention to increase the students' metacognitive processes; an awareness of their own learning and progress.

The third critical feature of the new paradigm is that it provides parents and members of the community with access to a wide variety of information concerning school, health, and social services. It is becoming more apparent that children will face an increasingly complex array of physical, psychological, emotional, and social problems that may inhibit their ability to learn. By giving parents and community members direct access to the knowledge-base, they may readily acquire knowledge about: (a) the availability of services provided by the school and local and state service agencies; (b) their child's academic progress, behavior, and assignments; (c) tactics for supporting learning at home and promoting their child's growth and development; and (d) school-related organizations and activities. This system would also allow school staff to communicate with parents and family members on a regular basis.

Although the new instructional paradigm is an essential component of SY2000, it represents only one aspect of schooling. The following section describes an entire system of schooling—the operations model—as defined by SY2000.

**The Operations Model**

Figure 4 presents a graphic description of the SY2000 Operations Model. It contains ten interrelated subsystems that work, in collaboration with families, the community, businesses and industry, and state and local agencies, to accomplish the mission. Each subsystem name is in one of the boxes. The model is designed as a set of interdependent and interrelated functions acting together to accomplish a predetermined purpose. Assessments of system elements are used in an iterative process to implement the continuous improvement program. The following is a brief description of each component of the SY2000 operations model.

*Research and Development*

We compared education's annual investment in research and development to that of successful businesses and industries and found that education invests trivial amounts of resources to produce future improvements. Perelman (1989) reported that the education sector spends only about 0.025 percent of its annual

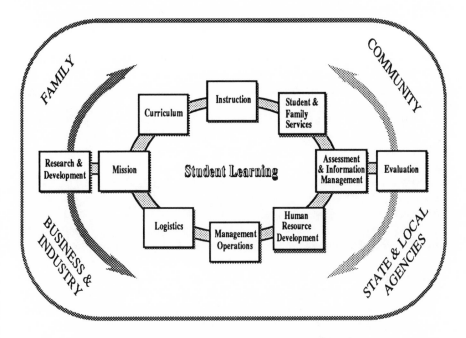

Figure 4. The Operations Model used in SY2000.

budget on research and development. This compares to an overall industry average in the United States of about 3.4 percent ranging from a low of 0.9 percent in containers and packaging industries to as much as 35% of gross revenues in high-tech industries such as telecommunications. With no significant investment in research and development, it is not difficult to see why education has changed so little over the past 100 years. The function of the Research and Development Subsystem is to acquire new knowledge related to all educational and management practices to assure that this knowledge is continuously put into the system.

*Mission*

The Mission Subsystem applies the principles of concurrent design to build community support and consensus on goals. The function of the mission process is to identify and articulate a vision that has two characteristics: first, it can be endorsed by a large number of the participants; and, second, it is self-renewing in the sense that the mission can be constantly improved and revised without disrupting the entire system.

We operationally define the mission of SY2000 to be that of preparing students to pass the significant adult assessments of life. That is, students will be prepared to pass college admissions examinations, employer selection tests, military selection tests, tests for admission into vocational programs, and to show mastery of the essential life skills, including personal communication, conflict mediation and resolution, and the requirements of citizenship.

*Curriculum*

Curriculum planners for SY2000 must assure that: (a) the curriculum supports the goals and objectives derived from the mission process, (b) curriculum areas complement and build upon each other, (c) information is organized to enable learners to achieve desired curriculum outcomes, and (d) assessment and instruction matches curricular content. A systematically balanced approach to teaching, learning, and assessment will facilitate the use of alternative approaches to schooling in SY2000.

Curriculum—what students need to know and be able to do—serves to fulfill the purposes of schooling. In SY2000, where the focus is on independent student learning, the curriculum serves as a guide to the learner and those assisting the learner (Banathy, 1991). The content and parameters of curriculum are specified in terms of learner outcomes that are derived from the mission. The master plan for curriculum provides descriptions of programs and courses of study integrating content, skills, and strategies across subject-area disciplines designed to support a continuous progress approach.

*Instruction*

Instruction is viewed as the intentional arrangement of conditions in the environment to facilitate attainment of identified goals (Driscoll, in press). It consists of activities designed to facilitate student attainment of curriculum goals and component objectives. Activities include direct purposeful experiences, simulations, demonstrations, mediated instruction, and interactions with databases and documents. Each learning outcome or integrated group of outcomes is matched with a number of different instructional activities, all of which are designed to facilitate student attainment of the desired goals. Within this framework, students are assisted in the selection of learning activities that best accommodate their current needs, abilities, and interests. Where appropriate, students are directed towards cooperative learning activities where there is an opportunity for meaningful social interaction.

Recent advances in knowledge engineering and knowledge database construction make it possible to organize the knowledge database for usefulness and learning rather than for teaching. This area of study, known as electronic performance support systems (EPSS), provides information to the student at the time of need ("just in time"), rather than according to a group schedule. The EPSS make it far easier to relate information or knowledge in one discipline to other fields (Gery, 1991).

*Assessment and Information Management*

Assessment is defined as the collection of data to verify performance, identify problems, and aid in decision-making (Salvia & Ysseldyke, 1988). The terms *assessment* and *evaluation* are frequently used as synonyms in educational settings to mean activities associated with rating the performance of students or educational programs. In Schoolyear 2000, the terms are used differentially. Assessment is confined to activities used to measure and appraise performance and to determine the status of all individual and system performance factors. Evaluation uses data collected by assessment for the appraisal of programs and can take place on a variety of levels, including the national level. Data gathered through continuous assessment procedures make it possible to identify strengths and weaknesses of individual learners and the system as a whole. In SY2000, the Assessment and Information Management Subsystem incorporates all data collection into a single subsystem. It deliberately includes regular data collection efforts typically associated with management information systems as well as individual student progress and performance data. The output of assessment is used to manage the continuous improvement program.

*Logistics*

It is our perspective that a significant reason for the limited success of the vast majority of educational innovations is that support structures were inadequate. Most education innovations have simply been add-ons to the current system. Thus, when political and economic climates change, support for the innovation often dissolves. We believe it is essential to design a logistics subsystem to address issues of supply, support, maintenance and repair, and acquisition of new systems.

The design of the Logistics Subsystem reflects the support needs which emerge from other subsystems and functions. These support needs may be for materials, goods, or services. It is the function of Logistics to assure that required resources are available when needed.

*Human Resource Development (HRD)*

Other innovations have failed in education because staff development procedures were not adequate. Fundamental to SY2000 is the requirement that all staff members be adequately prepared to perform all assigned tasks. Preliminary job analyses suggest that many jobs assigned cannot be performed within the context of normal operations. Bowsher (1989) pointed out that the job of teacher in traditional school organizations is not an embraceable responsibility; it is so complex that it cannot be done properly within existing organizations by even the top ten percent of the practitioners. Jobs must be designed for existing people; people must be prepared to perform the jobs.

A significant part of HRD resources in SY2000 will be invested in maintaining EPSS for all staff members. Because laws, curricula, assessment methodologies, and other factors are constantly changing, keeping materials and people up-to-date becomes a logistics nightmare. Consequently, new methods of staff performance development must be adopted. The entire areas of preservice and inservice training must be reconceptualized in light of technological advances.

Implementing leadership training programs that will prepare managers for new leadership roles and functions in a significantly different organization will be a continuing challenge for the HRD subsystem.

*Management Operations*

Management operations is the SY2000 term for what has been traditionally called administration. In one sense, all other subsystems are a part of management operations. We believe that it is necessary to redesign management operations, primarily because current operating models have evolved rather than been designed. With the introduction of quality systems and computerized information, decision-making information is made available to all staff, thus enabling a new organizational structure. Further, the system must be designed to be operated effectively by those we can reasonably presume to hire. Thus, to design a system that has appropriate supporting structures is critical to the general improvement of education.

The management operations subsystem takes into account modern practices in organizational design and work assignments. Contemporary concepts in organization design, task allocation, team coordination, and other work-enhancing methods provide the basis for SY2000 management. In combination with the organization design process, management operations identifies methods to reallocate existing resources to high-priority programs.

The organization design effort that creates the operations and management system must address explicitly issues influencing the quality of working life (Rosow & Yeager, 1989). SY2000 views students as members of the total working community, not just targets of service. This role reconceptualization requires that the quality of the student's working life be taken into account with the same vigor as with other members of the organization. We see that a wide range of governance, individual planning, and student contribution issues are critical to the success of a SY2000 program.

The leadership implications for SY2000 are profound. It is our full intention to move from a power-based, information control, leadership style to an information-based shared leadership style. We contend that this change requires much more than a simple redistribution of power. Traditional school-based and site-based management programs are classically suboptimal; no consideration for total system operations is typically found. We believe that the integration of a quality system and an accurate, up-to-date information system will improve the decision quality on a system-wide basis.

With substantial role changes for students, teachers, and administrators required to implement the new paradigm, why would any of them choose to adopt the new model? We find that there is a considerable frustration among all parties with the current model. Students are required to sit in rows and be quiet; teachers spend much of their time maintaining order; administrators must deal with numerous discipline cases that are caused by the role of inactivity imposed on students. These groups repeatedly express an intense interest in doing a better job. We sense a climate receptive to change, provided that no single group is made the scapegoat or is required to bear the entire burden.

*Student and Family Services*

The term "student and family services" is used to describe an array of services that will support learners to achieve curricular requirements. In SY2000, student and family services function as an integral component of each student's learning experience, which includes orientation, registration, academics, therapeutic and career counseling, placement services, maintenance and transfer of student records, acting as home-school liaisons, and providing student progress and behavior reports. Other services include, but are not limited to: physical, psychological, and social and developmental screenings, interventions, treatments and evaluations; suicide, alcohol, drug, and dropout prevention programs; and information and referrals to specialized educational programs and community resources. Currently, the role of student services continues to move toward a broader range of services, especially in the areas of health and social services, by coordinating and collaborating with public and private health and social service agencies.

Two principles put it succinctly: If we are to care for the child, we must care for the family. If we are to care for the family, we must reach out to the community. Academic goals can not be reached for all students unless we help our community address social and economic needs. Given the cross-functional impacts and mutual dependence in striving to achieve common goals, collaboration is, in fact, in the systems' own self-interest.

*Evaluation*

The Evaluation Subsystem monitors internal programs as well as external conditions to make necessary revisions to the total system. Ongoing results produced by the new system are constantly monitored, and revisions are suggested to assure that goals are being reached. This model assumes that if students are not learning, one or more of the components of the system are not working. Appropriate revisions are then made in the system to fix the problem.

The evaluation subsystem recommends revision priorities based on operational data.

A new concept related to evaluation arises from the design and implementation of quality systems for education. It appears that a quality system, as later described in this chapter, will replace most of the functions traditionally carried out under the titles of "educational evaluation," "program evaluation," or "institutional research." The implementation of a basic quality system takes care of about 95% of functions and activities traditionally assigned to evaluation. The part that is not done by the basic quality system is the segment that evaluates the effectiveness of the entire organization and its position in the marketplace. This relationship between quality systems and evaluation is currently being explored. Thus, for the purposes of this chapter, evaluation is illustrated as a subsystem function, and quality systems are viewed as a system process.

**System Processes**

The operations model in Figure 4 describes functions that each subsystem performs in the total system context. There are, however, important processes that cannot be defined as separate subsystems because they influence the operation of the entire system. The three key processes are: electronic systems, financial modeling, and quality systems. The following is a brief description of these processes.

*Electronic Systems*

Increases in speed, capacity, and capability of electronic systems, combined with dramatic decreases in cost, make possible designs that would have been impossible in the past. One fundamental assumption of the SY2000 design is that electronic systems will displace costs, not simply add to an existing cost structure.

Accordingly, electronic systems will be designed to support and enhance the operations of all of the subsystems. There are three broad areas of functionality. The electronic systems include: (1) communications, (2) an intelligent database, and (3) learning management systems. All of these must work together in a seamless manner.

**Communications.** Communications will be a central function of electronic systems. A generalized schematic diagram, developed by Gaede (1992), of the communications structure is included as Figure 6. At the most fundamental level, the electronic systems transport data objects from one location to another within learning sites, between learning sites in a district, between districts, and beyond. These data objects may be text files, binary applications or data files, digital audio or video images, or a combination of these. It should make no

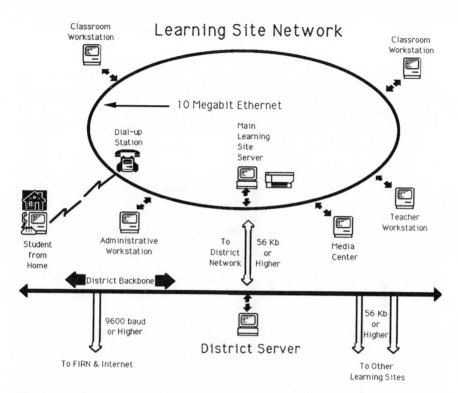

Figure 6. Schematic of the Communications and Data Network for SY2000.

difference to the communications structure what kind of object is being transported.

**Intelligent Database.** A second major area of functionality systems will focus on access to information access. The system should make it easy for students, teachers, or parents to access information from anywhere on the network, including from home workstations that are connected to the network. The system should be capable of accessing resources that are on the local area network or which are located at other sites. The database is organized for ease of use and contains routines that assist the users in accessing and using information.

**Learning Management System.** The learning management system will form the keystone of the learning process. It will have three component systems: (1) an electronic performance support system, (2) an expert tutoring system, and (3) a student records management system. In the typical mode of operation, a student will sign onto the system; the system responds by accessing student records and providing the list of available options, including several curricula, and can choose the desired area of study. The student may elect to take a diagnostic test, report on a completed assignment, take a performance examination, schedule an appointment with a teacher, or any of a number of other options. The final step in any single session will generally be the generation of an individually prescribed assignment, based on information which has previously been entered into the system.

A conceptual schematic of the overall electronic systems, developed by Gaede (1992), is included as Figure 7.

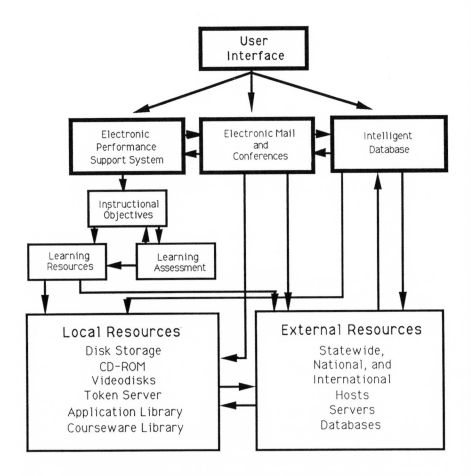

Figure 7. Schematic of Electronic Systems Used in SY2000.

*Financial Modeling*

Financial modeling provides the basis for optimizing system operations. The best estimates of future available funding for education indicate a declining portion of total state revenues. Consequently, it is necessary now, more than ever before, to plan optimum resource allocation. A prevailing characteristic of immature systems is that of sub-optimization of resources yielding uneven and often unpredictable outcomes. The resource allocation and financial simulation model for SY2000 is the Interactive Financial Planning System (Execucom Systems Corporation, 1984) adapted specifically to plan the design, development, implementation, and operation of the model.

The financial planning model will permit a carefully considered, though often approximate, estimate of the relative cost and relative value of alternative designs. This function, called design to cost, requires systems to meet predictive cost goals before they are adopted.

*Quality Systems*

A third process that applies to all operational functions is quality systems. As used in SY2000, quality is consistent with the international definition, "The totality of features and characteristics of a product or service that bear on its ability to satisfy stated or implied needs." A quality system is one that meets the requirements of national or international standards (e.g., ANSI 90 series; the ISO 9000 series—see Marquardt, 1991). Because quality is often used as a variable, practitioners often become defensive when it is suggested that they do not have a "quality" system. Unfortunately, the popular literature often confuses the term "quality" as intended by professionals with the term "excellence" as it is used by the public. Here, the operational definition of quality is a category, not a variable; one has a quality system in place, or one does not.

The goal of the quality system is to cause a student's accumulated performance record to conform to curriculum requirements. Control of the service-product quality requires quantitative data from written performance records as well as qualitative data collected from judgments made about the usefulness, esteem, and cost values of the service-product. Control of the service-product quality also requires control of failure costs associated with corrective action for students who do not meet reasonable curricular requirements, as well as the costs to society when the corrective action is not effective. Finally, the quality of all processes that affect the quality of the service product must be controlled.

One of the more difficult concepts for educators to understand and accept, is what we refer to as the first law of quality:

***Quality cannot be inspected into a product or service.***

Converted to education, it should say: "Quality cannot be tested into an educational program." We have often debated this issue with colleagues at the university who claim to have high standards for their courses. Operationally, this means that they tend to give low grades and fail a high proportion of their students. Since education, as measured by test scores, is a process representing the combined outputs of student and instructor efforts, the setting of an exceptionally high criterion does not improve the *processes* that cause success or failure. If one wishes to change the output of a system, one must change the processes that cause the output; not the method used to measure it.

There is probably no more profound body of knowledge critical to modern leadership than that of quality systems. Although leadership fashions come and go, quality systems are fundamental to making continuous improvements in any operating system. The adoption of ISO 9000 does not require a fundamental change in management philosophy as does the adoption of total quality management. Educational leaders would distinguish themselves by learning about and introducing quality systems in their districts.

Perhaps an example would be helpful. One requirement of quality systems is the documentation of work processes. In a Florida district, one function selected to introduce quality systems was that of the zone variance process. When students wish to move from one school to another in a district that is under a court order or consent decree, they must obtain a zone variance. How these are initiated and approved can be a significant bureaucratic tangle. In the district in question, it was found that 13 different individuals had to approve and that at least eight letters were sent out. By using process documentation software available for quality systems, the number of letters was cut to two and the number of approvals reduced to three, dramatically reducing the cost and time in the zone variance process.

The critical leadership issue to be gained from this example, and from the quality literature, is that these savings are not due to local heroes or personally outstanding gifted leaders; they are caused by applying carefully researched and practice-based procedures that can work for anyone who applies them with integrity. Of all the important lessons to be learned from the quality literature, the most important is that improvements can be continuously made by regularly employed administrative staff and faculty of the kind that can normally be expected to be hired.

**The Conflict Between Democracy and Design**

Educational administrators and researchers far removed from daily classroom practices have a long history for initiating top-down solutions to education (Cuban, 1990). These solutions have had little impact on traditional classroom practices and are typically spurned by educational practitioners who have been asked repeatedly to implement new programs with little time, training, or support. Few top-down strategies are faithfully implemented because they are not owned by the end-users and because they often fail to consider the pragmatics of daily school routine. Professional system designers, who have the capability to design new operational systems, have little chance for success without the collaboration of the school personnel. To achieve acceptance of the SY2000 design, we have adopted a new process to be described next.

*Principles of Concurrent Design*

Concurrent design has five major features and an operational methodology that differs from traditional linear models of systems design.

(1) *Address all levels of the organization simultaneously.* To do that requires assigning the major responsibility for design to an agency external to the operational units. This organizational structure permits the external agency to acquire performance requirements from all organizational levels simultaneously (see Morgan, 1989).

(2) *Obtain performance requirements from all stakeholders.* These include students, parents, business, industry, post-secondary education, teachers, administrators, and others. Each stakeholder should have the right to put forth performance requirements.

(3) *Reconcile differences in requirements.* Reconciliation of differences in performance requirements must be highly process driven. If it is only power driven, as in the case with most educational reforms, it will not be implemented with integrity.

(4) *Provide iterative design review.* These requirements must then be designed into the system. This review must be done openly, with frequent explanation of the process.

(5) *Establish a process of continuous improvement.* To achieve the goal of continuous improvement, one must first reach consensus on the processes to be employed, then document those processes carefully, then implement the processes with integrity.

## Conclusions

The leadership implications inherent in the SY2000 model are profound. First, in reconceptualizing the role of students as that of participants or knowledge workers means that their interests must be taken into account in any organization structure. Providing workers with the tools and support they need to get their jobs done and the inspiration and guidance to do them well becomes an important part of the leader's job.

Second, the style of leadership must change considerably since the information database will provide access to all forms of information required for daily performance and system improvement. We have searched for an analogy to describe the leader's role in SY2000. Currently, we think that the role of the leader is more like that of a quarterback; someone who is involved and working together with the remainder of the players.

Changes in the organization design and role definitions will lead to periods of turbulence and resistance to change when traditional power relationships are disturbed. By providing all stakeholders with information and an opportunity to have their concerns taken seriously, we hope to overcome the difficulties that new leadership requirements will bring to the system. New skills will be required in consensus building and priority setting, in which a proactive style replaces the typical reactive posture.

## References

Banathy, B. H. (1991). *Systems Design of Education: A Journey to Create the Future.* Englewood Cliffs, NJ: Educational Technology Publications.

Bowsher, J. E. (1989). *Educating America: Lessons Learned in the Nation's Corporations.* New York: John Wiley & Sons, Inc.

Branson, R. K. (1988). Why the schools can't improve: The upper limit hypothesis. *Journal of Instructional Development, 10*(4), 15–26.

Branson, R. K. (1990, Apr.). Issues in the design of schooling: Changing the paradigm. *Educational Technology, 30*(4), 7–10.

Bush, G. (1992, July 21). *Remarks by the President to Forum on Educational Choice.* Archbishop Ryan High School, Philadelphia, PA. Washington: The White House.

Chubb, J. E. & Moe, T. M. (1990). *Politics, Markets & America's Schools.* Washington, DC: The Brookings Institution.

Cuban, L. (1990). Reforming again, again, and again. *Educational Researcher, 19(1),* 3–13.

Driscoll, M. P. (in press). *Psychology of Learning for Instruction.*

Execucom Systems Corporation (1984). *Interactive Financial Planning System Users Manual Release 10.0.* Austin, TX: Author.

Firestone, W. A., Fuhrman, S. H. & Kirst, M. W. (1989, Oct.). *The Progress of Reform. An Appraisal of State Education Issues* (CPRE Research Report Series RR–014).

Gaede, O. (1992, June). *Description of the Proposed Electronic Systems for Schoolyear 2000.* (Available from the Center for Educational Technology, 406 MCH B–150, Florida State University, Tallahassee, Florida 32306.)

Gery, G. J. (1991). *Electronic Performance Support Systems.* Boston, MA: Weingarten Publications, Inc.

Gwartney, J. D. (1990). A positive proposal to improve our schools. *The CATO Journal, 10*(1), 159–173.

Lemann, N. (1991, January). A false panacea. *The Atlantic,* 101–105.

Marquardt, D. (1991, May). Vision 2000: The strategy for the ISO 9000 Series Standards in the 90s. *Quality Progress, 24*(5), 25–31.

Morgan, R. M. (1989). Systems design and educational improvement. In D. W. Chapman and C. A. Carrier (Eds.). *Improving Educational Quality: A Global Perspective.* Westport: CT: Greenwood Press (Praeger).

National Commission on Excellence in Education. (1983). *A Nation at Risk.* Washington, DC: United States Government Printing Office.

Perelman, L. J. (1989, Oct.). *Closing Education's Technology Gap.* Indianapolis, IN: The Hudson Institute, Herman Kahn Center. [See Chapter 12.]

Perelman, L. J. (1990, May). *The "Acanemia" Deception.* Indianapolis, IN: The Hudson Institute, Herman Kahn Center.

Rosow, J. M. & Yeager, R. (1989). *Allies in Educational Reform: How Teachers, Unions, and Administrators Can Join Forces for Better Schools.* San Francisco: Jossey-Bass.

Salvia, J. & Ysseldyke, J. E. (1988). *Assessment in Special and Remedial Education (4th ed.).* Boston: Houghton Mifflin Company.

Shanker, A. (1988, Nov.). *Proceedings of the School Year 2020: An International Seminar on Creating Effective Schools of the Future.* Snowmass, CO, p. 27.

Smith, C. S. (1981). *The Costs of Further Education: A British Analysis.* Oxford: Pergamon Press.

## About the Authors

*Robert K. Branson* is the Director of the Center for Educational Technology at Florida State University. Dr. Branson has twenty years of involvement in the design and development of large-scale, technology-based systems in education and training. He received his Ph.D. from Ohio State University.

*Atsusi Hirumi* is a Program Specialist with the Schoolyear 2000 project. He received his M.A. in educational technology from San Diego State University and is currently a doctoral candidate in Instructional Systems at Florida State University.

# 8/ Leadership for Transition: Moving from the Special Project to Systemwide Integration

## Betty Collis & Jef Moonen

### University of Twente

*This chapter considers the role of educational leadership in the overall process of computer applications in education. This process is characterized as having three general phases: (1) initial experimentation and enthusiasm, (2) special-project activity, and (3) integration into the ongoing practice of the teacher and the institutionalized system that supports this on-going practice. In particular, we expand on one particular aspect of this overall leadership—the transition between the special-project phase and the systemwide-integration phase—and argue that leadership for this transition presents a particular challenge. We illustrate the general argument with a case study from The Netherlands and relate the experiences from the Dutch national-level project to those encountered by the school principal. We conclude with considerations for the school leader with respect to leadership for helping staff to make the transition between special tryouts with computers in education and integration into daily practice.*

The use of computer-related technology for educational purposes is now widely accepted in educational systems throughout the world. The initial motivations for computers in education have been generally based on high expectations relative to what computer use might be able to do for the student, school, educational system, curriculum, or even the national economy (see Anderson & Collis, 1992, and Hawkridge, 1991, for analyses of these different motivations and the effect these motivations have on subsequent policy with respect to computers in education).

In practice, and speaking very generally, the pattern of experience with computers in education is a three-step process, each of which has roots in the vision of what computer use can finally effect in the educational system. The first step involves uncoordinated, individualistic initiatives fueled by some sort of vision or personal excitement about the potential impact of computers in education. These initiatives may be at the grassroots level or may be higher in the decision-making hierarchy, even at the top of it. Through the momentum of these initiatives, the second step in the process is typically some sort of special project, in which extraordinary time, money, and support is given to some exploration of or stimulation of computer use in schools. The desired eventual outcome of these projects, implicitly or explicitly, is systemwide diffusion. This third phase in the process involves, finally, implementation into the on-going routine of the teacher and institutionalization into the stable delivery process of school affairs. Figure 1 gives a simple visualization of this process that we will use as an organizer for the rest of this chapter and in particular that we will relate to the on-going leadership task of the present-day school administrator.

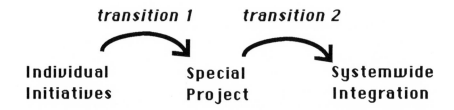

Figure 1. Simple View of the Process of Computer-use Diffusion in an Educational System.

We can identify this process from the national perspective, in many examples from centralized educational systems where special projects can be nationwide in character and systemwide integration can refer to the wide spectrum of subsystems involved in total educational delivery. These include those subsystems relating to teacher training, curriculum development, and resource supply and evaluation (see Collis & Oliveira, 1990, for an analysis). These large-scale national-level special projects generally only happen once for a particular innovation such as computers in education.

However, the process diagrammed in Figure 1 is not just a one-time affair, but can repeat itself on a smaller scale at the regional and school levels and even at the individual-teacher level, where the evolution from "good idea" to "special project or tryout" to "integration-into-daily-life" can begin any number of times.

At all these levels this diffusion process most frequently never makes it to completion of the integration-into-daily-life phase. Any number of surveys and analyses support this last statement, not only for computers in education but for innovations in general in education. White (1990), for example, describes the success rate for implementation of innovative programs beyond the special project phase as "very low...only about 20 percent" (p. 207) and supports this by an analysis of studies beginning in the 1970s. Fullan (1982) describes this as the problem of continuation and notes that when special funding ends very few special projects continue. Jansen and Vegt (1991) describe institutionalization as the situation when the delivery of education as well as school practice seems to be permanently altered so that an innovation is absorbed in a stable way into the life of the school. They, too, note that this "durable establishment of the new" frequently does not occur:

> Many attempts at educational innovation, whether they arise inside or outside the school, do not succeed. Renewal plans that were initially received with good intentions are in the end not integrated into the school. Alternatively, the essential nature of the innovation can be eroded: with small, almost imperceptible, alternations the school "tames" the renewal. (p. 33)

Pelgrum and Plomp (1991) in their analysis of computer use in 19 educational systems worldwide are among many who document this same sort of stalled process with respect to computers in education, both in terms of systemwide institutionalization for delivery and support but also in terms of integration into the teacher's daily practice. Despite undoubted individual enthusiasms and large-scale projects succeeding in bringing computers into schools throughout the world, the "final" step of teachers incorporating these computers into daily practice is far from being accomplished. The ambitious motivations of those who champion computers in education, as well as the requirements of those who are beginning to demand accountability for the considerable amounts of money that have been spent on computers in education, are often not being realized.

The purpose of this article is to consider the role of educational leadership in this overall process of computer diffusion in education and to suggest how that leadership can increase the chance of systemwide integration. In particular, we wish to expand upon one particular period of leadership challenge—that of the transition between the special-project phase and the systemwide-integration phase. This period has been labelled Transition 2 in Figure 1. We begin by considering the diffusion process through an examination of policy and leadership at the national level and then apply this examination to the ongoing task of the school principal.

Thus, the remainder of this chapter will take the following form. First, more illustration will be given of what is meant by "special project" and "systemwide integration" and the transition between them with respect to computers in education, in order to clarify the frames of reference of the terms. Next, a case study from The Netherlands will be given that illustrates the diffusion process from Figure 1. This case study will serve as a concrete example of the overall problem space for leadership relative to computers in education and in particular to leadership for the transition between special project and systemwide integration. Following this, the relationship between the case study from The Netherlands and the role of the school principal will be discussed, and particular issues related to leadership for transition such as the implications of moving too quickly or waiting too long relative to the transition between special project and systemwide integration will be considered. Finally, some suggestions and strategies will be given for school decision-makers with respect to leadership relative to computers in education within their schools.

Throughout the chapter for convenience we use the term "computers" to include the larger category of computer-related technologies such as multimedia and telecommunications-related resources as well as the more familiar stand-alone units. Also, when we talk about the national level, we mean the highest level of educational organization for a particular system. While in the majority of countries in the world this is the national level, in some countries such as the US, Canada, and Germany the frame of reference is the state, provincial, or local level. For convenience we will use "national" to refer to this highest level of organizational influence.

## Leadership Relative to the Special Project, Systemwide Integration, and the Transition Between Them

Figure 1 identified three phases in the diffusion process of computers in education. In this section some overall considerations relative to leadership within this diffusion process are outlined before moving to the case study from The Netherlands and the subsequent discussion relative to the role of the school principal. For convenience in the following remarks, the frame of reference is the national level, but as will be argued later the same process and issues affect leadership at the regional and school level. Leadership is not considered to be an explicit part of the process at the first, individual-exploration phase of the diffusion process so the discussion that follows focuses on the second and third phases of the process and the transition between them. Of course, even during the individual-exploration phase, educational leadership plays an important contribution in terms of endorsing the atmosphere for individual exploration within a system in which personal enthusiasms can grow.

**The Special Project**

In the "Special Project" approach to computer-related use in education, exploration with technology is carried out in a special environment, special with respect to quantity and quality of personnel, equipment, expectation, or other resources relative to average local standards. A typical strategy in the special project is to bring together a strong collection of players, all of whom share a commitment to the technology potential, and give these players extra time and resources to work out their ideas. Often, in the special-project philosophy, there is a conviction that the best talent should be supported and also that this talent needs central support to establish itself before, eventually, the system is able to handle responsibility for implementation itself. Sometimes, however, special projects deliberately look for a more representative setting, willing to serve as a testbed for new ideas. Often, special projects have some kind of a "installation-related" goal, such as to supply a certain number of computers to every school of a certain type or a certain amount of computer-related teacher training to a certain group of teachers (Collis & Carleer, 1992).

Explicitly or implicitly, the special projects are expected eventually to be of value to the remainder of the system not involved in the project, through demonstrating examples or through providing the strength, infrastructure, and shelter to allow a critical mass of experience and acceptance to develop (capacity building), so that the technology use can eventually support itself unaided.

There are many examples of the special-project approach at the national, regional, and school levels. At the national level, virtually every country in Europe has had a special project to stimulate computer use in schools where in principle all schools in the country would receive a basic infrastructure of equipment and experience. The case study from The Netherlands which follows later is an example of this kind of national-level project. The California Model Technologies Schools Project is an example of a special project at the regional level, in which a number of sites throughout the state have been given special resources in order to "demonstrate the effective use of technology in instructional delivery and enhancement," generating ideas and examples which can then be disseminated throughout the system (Matray, 1992). There are numerous examples of special projects at the school level. In the book, *Technology-Enriched Schools: Nine Case Studies with Reflections* (Collis & Carleer, 1992) details of 19 such school-based projects in six countries are discussed and analyzed. At the individual-teacher level, although less-well documented in literature, there are uncounted examples of the classroom teacher being stimulated by an idea relative to computer use, trying it out as a sort of individual special project, and then deciding if he or she wishes to make it an on-going part of instructional practice or not (see Kearsley, Hunter & Furlong, 1992).

Their characteristics ensure that most special projects take time and initiative to establish; typically "results" are not forthcoming for an extended period of time, often years; and the more partners involved the more complicated the project structure development. Also, special projects must have an infrastructure of their own, which often assumes the furtherance of their own existence as an unstated but parallel preoccupation of the special-project period. As the special project thrives or discovers it requires more resources to function, new leadership challenges emerge. "Thriving" can lead to more and more autonomous behavior, which can result in collisions of various sorts with overall system functioning.

The special project-approach requires a leadership philosophy attuned to experimentation and innovation. The leader needs characteristics appropriate to the task of making a team out of individuals from different backgrounds or component organizations. Thus, the leader must not be seen to be in conflict of loyalty him- or herself through parallel identification with one of the component organizations. Also, deciding on additional resource provision for a project in difficulty requires both evaluation and personnel-handling skills, as replacement of personnel or even project shutdown may be required, with the accompanying implications for those involved.

### Systemwide Diffusion

In contrast to the special project, the systemwide-diffusion orientation sees its goal as facilitating technology use throughout a system, not as a special object of attention but as a tool for handy use when and where appropriate, by teachers and students. Systemwide diffusion refers to both organization and content. Computer-related resources are to be handled as are other resources in the system as, for example, relative to purchasing and maintenance; are to be integrated into existing procedures for teacher training; and are non-exceptional variables within assessments of overall school functioning and performance. While not equating computers with other resources such as desks or textbooks or science laboratory equipment, systemwide integration would see the computer being as well integrated as books or the school library in the everyday practice of the school and teacher.

Many educational jurisdictions have this sort of systemwide integration as an explicit target for computer-related technology. This sort of integration is visible in the context of the new national curricula evolving in, for instance, The Netherlands, the United Kingdom, and Japan. It has emerged as a hoped-for goal in many of the North American states and provinces. And it is the long-term policy in many individual schools in countries in many different parts of the world.

Leadership relative to a systemwide diffusion model for technology in education also offers special challenges. One such challenge is finding strategies to informally evaluate the effective integration of technology within and between many different departments in the educational system (or the many different parts of the teacher's day) and to deal with the implications of different decisions when those decisions interfere with each other. This can happen, for example, when a curriculum committee may urge technology use as both a goal and tool for science laboratory use, but teacher trainers in science education may not wish to follow such an approach. Thus, time and resources spent in one department may come to little avail if not supported by another department. Leadership challenges here relate to maintaining the balance between fostering local control and preventing systemwide loss as a result of local decisions.

Another challenge relates to how to stimulate new ideas or potentialities related to rapidly emerging new technologies in a system-integration model. Institutionalization brings with it the characteristic of a certain freezing of an innovation (Jansen & Vegt, 1991) so that it can be fit to a routine, which runs the risk of soon having obsolete or no-longer-optimal characteristics of computer use entrenched in procedure. As an opposite danger associated with the rapid appearance of new possibilities with respect to technology in education, leadership in a systemwide model requires some level of central coordination, or else wide disparities may rapidly appear in the system (i.e., those responsible for hardware resources may move to a new type of computer without considering the implications for teacher training or curriculum resources that such a move may make).

Thus, in a systemwide integration approach, good leadership requires a capacity to keep well-informed about the developments within each component of the overall system and to identify when decision-making about technology use in one of these components will lead to conflict with the decisions or desires of other components. It requires the skill to know when and how to intervene in the procedures of suborganizations within the system to better shape coordination. Good leadership will also require a strategy for information dissemination throughout the system relative to new developments in technology for education, including both research and technical findings. Finally, good leadership in a systemwide approach will require the ability to identify appropriate persons to move into new "special project" leadership roles if an opportunity for a next round of special projects emerges.

## Transition Period Between Special Project
## and Systemwide Integration

While systemwide diffusion may be an eventual goal of special projects, there are many differences in the project approach and the systemwide-integration approach. Even if systemwide integration is centrally organized or stimulated, it carries with it the assumption of local control and decision making. The target end adopter is a member of a heterogeneous group—all the teachers in a system or school or other definable group—who will differ widely from one another in terms of prior experience with technology, interest in technology, or even interest in change and placement difficulties.

Lack of money and support at the previous project level will be generally the case, and "the larger the external resource support, the less likely the effort will be continued after external funds terminate, because the district cannot afford to incorporate the costs into its regular budget" (Yin, Herald & Vogel, 1977, p. 16). And in a heterogeneous setting, the system may not be willing to compensate for resource deficiencies by voluntarily putting in extra personal time or effort, as can generally be counted on in the "individual enthusiast" and "special project" phases. In addition, moving from the special project to integration will mean that those in the special project generally must move back into larger system again, which often brings many adjustment and placement problems and may result in the dissipation of the expertise of the project team.

All of these characteristics of the transition between the special project and systemwide integration call for special leadership skills from the administrator overseeing the transition process. Even with good leadership skills, bridging the transition period will be a challenge.

## Case Study in Educational Leadership with Respect to Computers in Education

In The Netherlands four periods of innovative activities with respect to computers in education can be distinguished: (a) before 1984: the era of the pioneers and grassroots developments; (b) 1984-1988: establishment of an innovative movement through the so-called unorthodox (special project) approach; (c) 1989-1992: blending of new policy about computers in education into the existing (non-computer specific) structures for the support of innovation in the educational system; and (d) 1993-upwards: systemwide integration (and new phases of innovation) within the autonomous school.

In the next paragraphs we will describe each of those periods. For each period the context, the leadership position, and the constraints relative to the computer-diffusion process will be described. A more complete description can be found in Plomp, Van Deursen & Moonen (1987).

### Grassroots Developments

*Context*

In The Netherlands innovation with respect to computers and education started as grassroots movements at the end of the 1960s. Projects were set up by individuals in order to explore the possibilities of the computer in educational practice and to improve particular aspects of educational practice. Projects were also set up at universities as only those organizations had access to the mainframe computers needed for some kinds of computer-based learning at that time. Some projects were conducted explicitly in the university environment; others connected university people and facilities and secondary or primary schools. At the end of the 1970s, when micro-computers entered Dutch life, many more individuals, particularly in schools, became pioneers in this area. Grassroots developments blossomed.

*Leadership*

Most of the time the didactic approach within a subject area at the university or school was the basis for starting exploration of using computers in education. Therefore, the leadership within such projects came from individual teachers or professors already trying to deal with those instructional problems. Leadership at a higher hierarchical level was no more than incidentally involved. The faculty deans or school principals accepted the pioneers' interest in new developments without taking any kind of leadership position in the area.

*Constraints*

The teachers involved had to deal with the problems they encountered at both the technical and organizational levels. Often the functioning and limited possibilities of the computer hardware and software created technical problems. The logistics needed for having computers available and acquiring expertise to deal with the technical problems involved created organizational problems. Because of the (non)leadership situation, many projects bounced against all kinds of practical constraints. But at the same time, a wave of enthusiasm about the great potential of computer technology for education came into existence.

The combination of individual enthusiasm, the growing importance of microelectronics, and the projected influence of microelectronics on society and on the economic developments of the country created a growing pressure on the Dutch government to take these grassroots developments seriously. As a result, committees were installed to prepare a national policy with respect to what was called "Information Technology and Education."

## The "Unorthodox Approach" (National-level Special Project)

*Context*

During the period 1980-1983 reports of special committees and discussions in the Dutch parliament led to the governmental decision that the use of computers in education needed a special centrally-led innovative effort. It was also decided that this innovative approach should be expressed through an even-larger special national project explicitly focused upon two goals: (a) to get each citizen acquainted with information technology, and (b) to create sufficient "human capital" to support the economy and the functioning of Dutch society in an emerging technologically oriented world. A large-scale project, called the Informatics Stimulation Plan (INSP), was set up as a four-year project (1984-1988).

Clearly, the projected innovation went far beyond simple educational objectives about using computers as didactic support in subject areas. The goals were explicitly related to broader issues such as economic and societal development. Taking as a starting point experiences abroad, the innovation set up a comprehensive set of activities involving special national (sub)projects related to computers and education: (a) the building up of a national and regional infrastructure for the development and distribution of educational software; (b) specific (sub)projects focused on the different educational sectors (elementary, secondary, and vocational education); (c) inservice training and information dissemination; (d) preservice training; and (e) research.

*Leadership*

In the Netherlands there is a national support structure consisting of six large and many smaller institutes whose regular task is to support educational innovations in primary and secondary schools. However, when this structure was created many years ago, the government did not realize that it, as with every organizational structure, was going to develop its own dynamics and therefore its own approaches and goals. As a consequence there were serious doubts that the existing structure for the supposed support of innovation in schools would be able to cope with the demands of the information technology innovation. First, to cope with this computer innovation meant being able to respond to specific pressure from society, which was different from the traditional entrance point of an educational innovation through strong curriculum-oriented links—the way the support structure had organized itself to work. Second, doubts occurred because there would be a large technological component involved in the innovation, which was not part of the current experiences of those in the support structure.

Also, because of the global approach that was taken, an additional set of problems was anticipated in terms of leadership. Traditionally, a Ministry of Education is divided into different directorates, each dealing with a specific area of the educational system or process. Given the global approach and the need to handle that approach in a concentrated way, the coordination of the many directorates within the Ministry of Education was expected to create problems that would require special skills and stature of those in the computers in education leadership.

As a result of this analysis, the Dutch government decided to create an ad-hoc, so-called unorthodox approach, with a limited lifetime, to initiate the computers-in-education innovation. As such the government could circumvent potential problems within its own Ministry and within the existing educational support system. In addition both the Ministry and the traditional support structure got the benefit of time to respond from within their existing organizations to the way the innovation evolved and to prepare to take over when, eventually, systemwide integration was expected.

The unorthodox approach was shaped by forming a special three-person management team within the Ministry. This team had direct links to the Minister himself and was made responsible for the total budget of the project. The management team showed strong leadership, not only because of their personal skills and characteristics, but also because the members of the team had no links to existing organizations whose interests they had to defend. As a counterpart of this management team, and outside of the Ministry, content- and sector-oriented management teams were set up, concentrated into positions for 10 to 11 project managers, augmented with a new (temporary) national institute to bring together special skills and expertise in the area of the application of information technology to education. Thus, in The Netherlands Transition 1 (relative to Figure 1) of the diffusion process was accomplished.

*Constraints*

This approach had many advantages. Suddenly, a substantial amount of resources and money became available to support the introduction of information technology into the schools. Central decision-making about hardware standards, about educational software development strategies, about the management of projects, and about the approach and content of teacher training were introduced. The introduction of computer literacy in the first years of secondary education became a great success through planned national strategies such as every secondary school receiving a networked set of 15 computers with a starter package of especially prepared software, and teacher training for three teachers per school (one of whom had to be a female) integrated directly with the hardware and software. And in the vocational education area, the provision of hardware and software improved the circumstances through which those schools could better cope with the new technological developments in the industries for which they were preparing students.

Although mentioned in the starting policy documents, an emphasis on introducing the computer as an instructional aid in education was not a major focus in the beginning of the project. However, as the project evolved, this focus began to get more attention in all of the specific activities. Then it became apparent that the integration of new didactic approaches into teacher practice were not so easy to realize: first because changing existing educational practice is always a difficult problem; and, second, because the leadership position of the INSP project was not fitted to stimulate such a change. This leadership was very well equipped to introduce a new topic such as computer literacy or to decide that the vocational education sector needed more hardware, because such decisions could to be taken on a national level. Decisions about changing classroom practice, however, needed the direct involvement of classroom teachers, as well as the involvement of the school principals not only for support of the teachers but also with respect to the organizational aspects about how to deal with equipment and its maintenance in the schools.

## PRINT: A Special Project for Transition Between Centralized Special Project and Systemwide Integration

*Context*

By 1986 it became clear that the continuation of the INSP should be based upon a different approach to educational leadership. Instead of providing hardware, software, and training infrastructure, the integration of information technology into the classroom became the central issue. A new national-level special project was defined: PRINT (Project for the Implementation of New Technologies), to be executed from 1989 until 1993. The organization of the PRINT Project was concentrated around three subprojects, each focused toward a specific educational sector (primary and special education, non-vocational secondary education, and vocational education). Within those subprojects three principal areas were identified: (a) computer-managed instruction and classroom management, (b) learning and application of information science and informatics, and (c) computer-assisted learning. Other major activities such as hardware provision, development of educational software, and teacher training still got plenty of attention, but now from a starting point within each educational sector itself.

*Leadership*

In his policy document (Deetman, 1988) the Minister of Education wrote that "further stimulation of educational development is a necessity, in which increasing the autonomy of the educational field will be a prior condition" (p. 3). As already foreseen at the start of the INSP, the integration by school principals and teachers should eventually take over. This was also one of the conclusions of an evaluation of the INSP that had been performed. In the evaluation report (Zegveld, Scheerens & Stehouwer, 1988) it was stated that: "... the emphasis should be placed more positively on stimulation from the demand side."

However, many teachers and school principals were not yet ready to take over this school-based leadership. Therefore, the leadership role for PRINT moved instead towards involving the existing support structure for innovation in The Netherlands as an interim step between the centralized special project and the expectation of school-based integration and leadership. It was hoped that the previously existing Dutch educational support structure had used the INSP years to prepare themselves for this leadership role. A project management team was formed, with representatives from each of the six major support organizations (organizations with a long history of competition among themselves for both ideological and financial reasons). Also, for each of the three educational sectors (elementary, secondary, and vocational) a special organizational team was set up to explicitly balance the power structure among the six support organizations. A management team was also put in place in the ministry, but with much less influence than had been the case in the INSP period, as the power had explicitly been shifted to the support organizations. Virtually none of the expertise from the INSP period continued on in leadership positions within PRINT, in that each of the component support organizations moved its own people into leadership roles.

Thus, in The Netherlands Transition 2 in Figure 1 became a four-year special project in its own right.

*Constraints*

Whenever the management of a major operation is changed, it takes time and effort to smooth out the difficulties and take out the rough edges of the transition. This natural phenomena also happened at the start of the PRINT Project. That was unfortunate, however, because it created a backlog of several months before the new leadership position was clearly established. That situation did not create a strong initial impression in the field of practitioners, which had already been generally critical for many years about the leadership capacity of the Dutch educational support structure with respect to educational innovations.

More substantially, however, the educational leadership position given to the support structure by the Ministry of Education, and in a way by the political powers in the Dutch parliament, was also challenged by other groups in the educational system, especially in the vocational education sector. In that sector interests were traditionally brought together within other organizations that did not relate to or participate in the official educational support system that was now responsible for PRINT. Their challenge of the PRINT leadership position was partly caused by lack of confidence in general in the educational support system—a lack of confidence which had almost become a traditional situation through its long history—but also by the too-bureaucratic approach executed by the new PRINT Project management itself. What should have been done through the leadership of PRINT, namely, to bridge the gap between a very centralized approach during the INSP and the strong involvement of the actors in the schools, did not really occur.

The impression developed that the leadership of the project was very much involved in strengthening its own position instead of thinking about the interests of the schools. It was therefore no surprise that in 1990 the Minister ordered an evaluation of the PRINT Project, with the (almost) expected result that strong criticism was formulated about the way it was led and managed. Consequently, a part of the project (the subproject that dealt with vocational education) was taken away from PRINT. A new organizational structure (called PRESTO) was created that had credibility in the vocational education sector and that took over the leadership position for that sector. Immediately PRESTO gave strong emphasis to input and influence from the vocational schools themselves. The remaining PRINT project (for primary and non-vocational secondary education) continued. However, the lesson was understood, and also in those subprojects more attention was given to schools and their actors.

Although the PRINT Project has not yet ended, it seems fair to say that it could not repeat the success of the INSP Project. When considering the three areas on which the project was focused (see above), only the second one (concerning the use of information science and informatics) remained successful. But that had already been the case in the INSP. In secondary education no breakthrough has occurred to anticipate teacher integration of computer-managed or computer-assisted learning. In the elementary sector, the large-scale implementation efforts started much later, so it is too early yet to have a clear opinion about the eventual success of integration of the instructional use of computing in that sector.

A crucial question, of course, is whether the lack of a clear success for PRINT is the result of a lack of adequate leadership. If yes, what leadership could have been provided to change the results? The obvious message is that the self-interests and prior competitive histories of the existing groups given key roles in the project predestined extreme difficulties for the project leadership. As a general impression, however, a stronger focus of the leadership towards the needs of schools and the existing conditions within the schools could have had some influence.

But by and large there probably would not have been a significant difference from the situation which did occur even if more school involvement had been offered. The main reason for this impression is based on the experiences of the PRINT successor (PRESTO) for vocational education. PRESTO has made considerable efforts to reach the schools and school actors. Nonetheless, the great majority of teachers did not respond to the invitations. It is the old story about people who do not want to change and/or do not have the time for it. In addition, new professional developments have taken the attention of the teachers, developments with respect to global organizational and content-oriented restructuring of their school system and a constant stream of arguments about their salary levels. In such circumstances no external leadership seems to be able to attract sufficient attention to stimulate a big move forwards in changing instructional practice using computers.

## Systemwide Integration: The Autonomous School

*Context*

When the PRINT Project ended in 1993, the government had prepared its policy about how to continue. Continuation could be done following one of two conflicting positions. On the one hand, the PRINT management argued very strongly that schools and school actors were still not able to take over the decision-making for integrating information technology into their own hands, and therefore a centrally-steered approach, with a centrally-organized leadership, was still necessary. On the other hand, it was argued that almost eight years had passed in which schools and school actors had had the chance to get acquainted with information technology and its potential, and that centrally-organized hardware provision, educational software development, and teacher training had been made generously available during this time. The infrastructure of the schools and its staff with respect to handling computers was rather well put into place. Therefore, it was up to the school now, given the means and resources, to make up its mind and decide in what way and in what amount information technology was going to be used.

After long discussion, the government decided to choose the latter approach. That approach fit into a more general movement that had become apparent in The Netherlands and that was being motivated by a cluster of reasons, political and financial as well as educational: the movement towards a more autonomous school. The major characteristic of this movement is to give the school what is considered as a reasonable budget, but then let the school choose its own priorities for the use of that budget.

*Leadership*

The choice of the government for the autonomous school policy clearly indicates that the leadership position now with respect to computers in education in The Netherlands has to shift toward the school principal and, finally, to the individual teacher. The school, and within the school the subject areas, have to become the central units where change has to occur. The main reason is that finding a balance between change efforts and the effects of the change process can best or perhaps only be done within each particular situation itself. It is only a school principal, knowing his or her school and its circumstances, that can decide if the time for change is right. The principal knows if the technological infrastructure of the school is sufficient. He or she knows about the level of expertise and motivation of the staff. He or she also has to decide if the school wants to cooperate with other schools in this area, and if it is wise to try to stimulate specific teachers or subject areas to get more involved.

The same reasoning is true at the subject-area level. Teachers themselves are the best judge about how deeply to become involved in instructional change in their own subject area.

By choosing this direction and by providing the necessary means, the Dutch government hopes that leadership for computers in education, once the province of the few pioneers, has reached enough teachers and school principals so that a critical mass has come into existence in a sufficient number of Dutch schools. Such schools should start a snowball effect, providing good examples of instructional computing practice. Thus, the leadership with respect to computer in education is brought back to the place were it belongs.

*Constraints*

Of course, there are many obstacles that could prevent success in this new leadership orientation. The main obstacle is a shift in interest away from computers among teachers in general because of their preoccupation with new policy issues more directly affecting their jobs and salaries. Although the government has a realistic budget available for the support of information technologies in schools, it is becoming visible that the strong interest in computers in education, which had been in schools for the last ten years, is fading. Because of this long period of time, this is a natural movement. At the same time, it is fair to notice that in society in general the impact of computerization has not lived up to its promises. Another obstacle is a growing negative attitude among teachers toward investing energy in innovations in general as a result of salary constraints.

## Issues Related to Leadership for Transition and Their Relationship to the School or District Administrator

The Dutch case study illustrates issues related to educational leadership relative to each phase of an attempted diffusion process for computers in education, beginning at the national level and moving finally into the schools as the focal point around which ultimate systemwide integration, if it is going to occur, must be wanted and steered. Therefore, because of his or her influence on the school, the school principal becomes a central figure in the integration phase of the diffusion process relative to computers in education, regardless of whether the special project preceding the integration phase was at the national, regional, school, or even individual-teacher level.

There has already been considerable analysis of the role of the school principal in facilitating continuation or integration of an innovation within the school. Fullan (1982) is one of the major sources of this analysis and within his well-known book many hundreds of pertinent associated references are given. For example, Fullan notes that the school principal becomes the key to continuation of the goals of a special project within the school once the project loses its funding and special status (see also Berman & McLaughlin, 1978; Leithwood & Montgomery, 1982; and Nicholson & Tracy, 1982). Therefore, the principal's leadership role in leading the transition between special project and schoolwide integration must be emphasized. Often, others are involved in this transition as well, especially if, as in the Dutch example, decisions about ending special project status are made at a level outside of the individual school. But, in any case, major issues for leadership involve identifying the right moment and pace for phasing out the special project and supporting systemwide integration. These and other issues are discussed next in a way that relates the Dutch case study to the experience of the school or district administrator outside of The Netherlands.

### What are the main issues from the Dutch case study that can relate to the leadership role of the school or district administrator?

Although there are differences in scale and in local particulars, the Dutch national-level case study offers a number of points of reference to the local administrator at the district or school level. There are a number of major lessons that have common relevance.

*What are key considerations in selecting project leaders?*

A first point of consideration relates to the composition of leadership needed for special projects. In the Dutch case, the key persons in the INSP Project were individuals carefully chosen for their personal leadership strength. They fulfilled their task without having to at the same time represent a particular group or institution (they were all from the Ministry). However, the key persons in the PRINT Project were individuals chosen to represent their home organizations in the project. Thus, the histories and personalities and jurisdictional issues that already were present in the interactions among those organizations were brought forward into the project venue and proved at times to be crippling. In the school or district this can also be a dilemma. Should committees and projects be set up with the "best" people, even if this leads to a lack of balance in terms of home institutions in project leadership? To what extent do members of a project team represent their home groups with regard to decision-making about the project? To what extent do prior considerations and relationships affect decision-making about computers-in-education activity? The Dutch example illustrates well the difficulties in trying to be democratic in terms of project organization.

*When is the right time for transition between the special project and systemwide integration?*

As the Dutch example illustrates, the answer to this question will vary depending on the perspective of who is being asked. In many cases, a project has a predefined timeframe, which appears to provide a simple answer to the transition-timing question, but as was seen in the Dutch situation, the end of one special project, such as the INSP, can be the beginning of another special project, such as PRINT, if the decision makers do not feel transition is appropriate. And at the end of PRINT in The Netherlands, many feel it is still too soon to move to school-based ownership, and would prefer another round of centrally supported special project initiatives.

But both moving too quickly and waiting too long can have negative consequences. Moving too quickly may mean that the system will resist taking ownership as appears to be happening in the vocational education sector in The Netherlands. Teachers will not yet be able to see the ways in which computers can be valuable in their teaching, or picture the ways in which they could use them in a routine or independent manner. And, even if they can, the support system they need in order to have computer use truly integrated into their work patterns may not yet be operable. Resource centers which have to handle computer resources as well as all their own materials may not have specialized staff able to deal with the technical problems surrounding continually changing hardware and software. Curriculum development teams may not have people with the experience and insight to appropriately align computer use with other instructional materials and curriculum. Teacher training and inservice deliverers may not have staff experienced in using computers in the classroom (a problem likely to continue for many years) so effective guidance and coaching and stimulation will continue to be lacking in the school-teacher education liaison (see Eraut, 1990, for consensus on the seriousness of this problem among ministers of education in Europe). Educational software may not be in adequate supply. All these factors together suggest that too-soon removal of the guidance and structure of the special project may leave computer use to occur only among the hearty pioneers who will push on regardless of lack of support.

Waiting too long can also have negative consequences. The special project can build up such an identity of its own that its disbandment will cause serious personnel and contractual problems. The reputations and benefits that have come to those in central positions in the special projects will be difficult to compensate for if they go back into the system. (This was an issue between the Dutch INSP and PRINT Projects.) Thus, they may leave the system entirely and take with them the expertise for which the system has paid so much for so long. Those in the schools will come to expect that all will be done for them and will lack the local leadership experience to know how and where to begin in managing their own affairs. Or, they may feel so disenfranchised from the decision-making of the special project that they begin to react negatively to whatever it does and subsequently may reject doing anything with computers in education as a sort of counterreaction, which is what has generally happened in the Dutch PRINT Project. Another problem which can come from waiting too long is that the initial excitement in a new area such as computers in education can fade away by the time that opportunities are finally made available for individual control of activities. Disillusionment can have set in and the sense of vision which is necessary to drive change is difficult to sustain over time. The feeling that "we tried that once and it was a disaster" is too easy to remember if schools and teachers are not challenged to keep going after initial trial experiences. The development of a human network of teachers sharing experiences and ideas with each other can be an important support mechanism. Special projects may be too limited in time and membership for this sort of networking to develop in a realistic sense. Waiting too long to give teachers ownership of an innovation can result in a missed opportunity for growth.

*How should transition be timed?*

Another major question is the timing of transition. Reasonably, it would seem sensible to have a gradual transition between special project and system integration, but in practice this becomes difficult to handle. Those in the special project who know their days are numbered naturally begin to invest more and more energy into where they as individuals or as a re-formed group will go next. In a transitional period in which decisions are made in more than one place, inevitable confusion and wastage may occur. Long periods of phasing out will likely exacerbate the negative aspects of "waiting too long" as described above, as the special project will probably become less and less effective in its role while still retaining formal control. In the Dutch situation, the second special project, PRINT, may have turned out to involve too long a transition time, in that the "waiting too long" dynamics described above, particularly that of the system as a whole loosing interest in computers, seems to be occurring.

*How should transition be managed?*

The above sets of problems relating to both the timing and pace of transition can be reduced through effective educational leadership during the transitional period. Expertise that has developed during the special project should be carried forward as much as possible into liaison or partnership roles with those who will be making decisions about computers if systemwide integration successfully does occur. Those in the system who will be taking over responsibility must be gently led to see that reinventing the wheel will not be as productive for them as learning from the experiences of those who worked within the previous special project. Stimulating this sort of mutual respect for each other's experience and point of view will be a major human-resource management task for the educational leader. Also, balancing the characteristics of the new situation with the historical baggage that preexisting groups bring with them into any new collaboration requires leadership and political sensitivity of a very high order.

*How do people's expectations of leadership change between the
special project and integration phases? How can these
changing expectations be handled during the transition period?*

During a special project, particularly during its formative and early days, its leadership is expected to be strong, aggressive, and to embody the identity of the project in order to give it recognition and respect. However, as a special project continues and its internal strength grows, this leadership style can turn into that of a "star" who comes to be resented by others even within the project who also wish part of the rewards of identification with the project. With the systemwide-integration approach, leadership must become much more subtle. Each group and subsystem has its own ways and local identity; nurturing a willingness to cooperate while not appearing to infringe on the local autonomy of a subsystem requires different sorts of leadership sensitivity. Skills for managing conciliation and leading others to accept suggestion grow in importance. Being well informed without appearing to be interrogating or overstepping one's authority is another special skill for leadership in an integrated system. And identifying the moment in which another special project can be started is another important leadership task. Putting the most appropriate persons into leadership roles in new special projects which emerge locally is particularly sensitive, as the various decision-makers in the different local subgroups will react very quickly to what they might perceive as an invasion on their procedures.

*What happens if the system isn't ready, after all, for integration?*

This is also difficult. One response is to move back to new special projects, but some of the difficulties in that were described above. More fundamentally, the overall system cannot afford to support integration being handled badly or which cannot hope to succeed because of local conditions. The strength to stop a process that is not productive is also part of the task of leadership and should be handled in a way that is both humane to those personally involved and not of potential long-term burden to the system. Making an unsuccessful project leader a "special advisor" to the minister may solve an immediate personnel problem, but will carry with it problems or at the very least wasteful expenditure to the system for many years to come.

Finally, we must trust the practitioner in his or her final judgment. If, after having adequate time and experience and support to become familiar with computers in education, the school chooses to put its priorities elsewhere, those who advocate systemwide integration of computers in education may have to graciously accept the lack of reception to their ideas. Or reshape their ideas until field interest and grassroots acceptance occurs.

## Suggestions and Strategies for School Decision-Makers

For the school decision-maker, what are the main points that can be taken from the discussion in this chapter? Perhaps the following:

1. Within your own school, look for opportunities to build upon local enthusiasm and exploration as the basis of special projects. Conversely, avoid special projects for which no real individual belief or commitment exists within the school.

2. Nurture a special project with extra time and resources. As those in the project gain confidence, look for ways to begin to link what they are doing with on-going processes in the school.

3. Be sensitive to the personal dynamics of all involved when moving away from the special project and toward systemwide integration. Build on the expertise of the early adopters, but also nurture others who, later on, begin to get involved.

4. Know when and how to stop a special project or the assignment of special responsibility to certain persons when those become counterproductive.

5. Keep well informed about who is doing what, and also about emerging possibilities for linkages and cross-fertilization among your staff and others.

6. Maintain established conventions for decision-making at the same time as giving more and more personal control.

7. Be alert for the start of new diffusion cycles and manage the development of new special projects in a way that minimizes conflict with locally established procedures.

8. Be aware of and respond creatively to "the central dilemma of the institutionalization process. On the one hand, 'stability through routinization' guarantees secure borders for the innovation, but, having so successfully refrozen, this contains the possibility of death-through-freezing. On the other hand, flexibility which encourages continuous interaction between the innovation and the host system—through permeable borders—constantly evokes modifications or revisions, leaving neither system nor innovation much opportunity to rest. This dilemma has been underanalyzed" (Jansen & Vegt, 1991, p. 45).

## References

Anderson, R. & Collis, B. (1992, April). *International Assessment of Functional Computer Abilities.* Paper presented at the annual meeting of the American Educational Research Association, San Francisco.

Berman, P. & McLaughlin, M. (1978). *Federal Programs Supporting Educational Change: Implementing and Sustaining Innovation. Vol. 8.* Santa Monica, CA: Rand Corp. (ERIC Document Reproduction Service No. ED 159 289).

Collis, B. & Carleer, G. (1992). *Technology-Enriched Schools: Nine Case Studies with Reflections.* Eugene, OR: International Society for Technology in Education.

Collis, B. & Oliveira, J. B. (1990). Categorizing national computer-related educational policy: A model and its applications. *Information Technology for Development, 5*(1), 45–68.

Deetman, W. J. (1988). *Policy Document for the OPSTAP Operation to Information Technology in Education in The Netherlands.* PSOI series nr. 36. Zoetemeer: Ministry of Education and Science.

Eraut, M. (1990). *Education and the Information Society.* London: Cassell Educational Ltd.

Fullan, M. (1982). *The Meaning of Educational Change.* Toronto, Ontario: OISE Press.

Hawkridge, D. (1991). Machine-mediated learning in third-world schools? *Machine-Mediated Learning, 3,* 319–328.

Jansen, T. & Vegt, R. van der. (1991). On lasting innovation in schools: Beyond institutionalization. *Journal of Educational Policy, 6*(1), 33–46.

Kearsley, G., Hunter, B. & Furlong, M. (1992). *We Teach with Technology: New Visions for Education.* Wilsonville, OR: Franklin Beedle Associates.

Leithwood, K. & Montgomery, D. (1982). The role of the elementary school principal in program improvement. *Review of Educational Research, 52*(3), 309–339.

Matray, K. (1992). California model technology schools: The Monterey perspective. In B. Collis & G. Carleer (Eds.), *Technology-Enriched Schools: Nine Case Studies with Reflections.* Eugene, OR: International Society for Technology in Education.

Nicholson, E. & Tracy, S. (1982). Principal's influence on teacher's attitude and implementation of curricular change. *Education, 103*(1), 68–73.

Pelgrum, H. & Plomp, Tj. (1991). *Computers in Education Worldwide.* Oxford: Pergamon.

Plomp, Tj., Van Deursen, K. & Moonen, J. (Eds.). (1987). *CAL for Europe: Computer Assisted Learning for Europe.* Amsterdam: Elsevier.

White, G. P. (1990). Implementing change in schools: From research to practice. *Planning and Changing, 21*(4), 207–224.

Yin, R., Herald, K. & Vogel, M. (1977). *Tinkering with the System.* Lexington, MA: D. C. Heath.

Zegveld, W. C. L., Scheerens, J. & Stehouwer, T. L. (1988). *An Initial Impetus: Report on a Sober, Forward-Looking Evaluation of the Information Technology Stimulation Plan.* PSOI Series nr. 46. Zoetemeer: Ministry of Education and Science.

## About the Authors

*Betty Collis* is a member of the Faculty of Educational Science and Technology at the University of Twente, The Netherlands. Prior to this, Dr. Collis was a member of the faculty of the University of Victoria, Canada, where she received her Ph.D. She has been involved in many different aspects of computer use in education and training, including software design and development, teacher training, curriculum development, and evaluation of effectiveness.

*Jef Moonen* is Dean and Professor of the Department of Educational Science and Technology at the University of Twente. Dr. Moonen has been involved in many aspects of computer applications in education and training, especially the development of national policy for information technology in schools. He received his Ph.D. from the University of Leiden.

# 9 / Technology Leadership in the English Educational System: From Computer Systems to Systematic Management of Computers

**Brent Robinson**

University of Cambridge, U. K.

*This chapter describes the evolution of information technology in the English educational system. Government policies and legislation have played a prominent role in the development of technology in English schools and resulted in a national curriculum for information technology. Changes in the roles and responsibilities of teachers, coordinators, and administrators due to the implementation of the information technology curriculum are discussed with particular attention to the nature of leadership required at different levels of the school system.*

## Introduction

To understand the nature of educational technology leadership in England at the present time, it is necessary to understand something of the unprecedented changes which have occurred within the English educational system—changes which themselves were brought about by leadership at a national level. Good leadership requires a sense of vision, and a critical element in technology leadership is the ability to develop and articulate a vision of how technology can produce change (Cory, 1990). In the 1970s there had been growing disquiet about the function of English education and its degree of success. In 1976 the Labour Prime Minister, James Callaghan, gave a speech at Ruskin College, Oxford questioning the function of English education. It was the start of what has become known as "The Great Debate."

One theme of disquiet which emerged was a failure by schools to prepare children for the world of industry and commerce. Two years later into The Great Debate, that theme was given a significant extra dimension when the British Broadcasting Corporation broadcast a television program *Now the Chips are Down*. It has long been rumored (Fothergill, 1988, p.21) that James Callaghan watched this description of silicon chips, their potential, and some of the possible consequences that would follow from their use. It appeared that schools were not equipping children well enough especially in information technology (IT). Here then was an educational problem; it had a technological answer requiring theoretical, political, and financial support structures to ensure its success. By 1980, despite a change of political party in power, the same view persisted and the Government had embarked upon a substantial microtechnology program for schools. On December 31st, a Conservative backbench MP wrote in The Guardian newspaper:

> Within a year or 18 months every secondary school should have a microcomputer. ... Several teachers from each school should undergo a Computer Assisted Learning course in the techniques and usage of computers. ... The aim should be that within three years every boy and girl who leaves school should be familiar with computers and associated technology, and have acquired a simple digital facility and some experience in using and understanding them.

Within a few weeks, that correspondent, Kenneth Baker, was promoted to a Ministerial post in the Department of Trade and Industry. He went on to become Secretary of State for Education and so began eight years of technological innovation in schools instigated by the Government through the Departments of Education and Industry.

## The Evolution of an IT Policy

During the 1980s, the Government continued to refine its vision. As a result of what teachers began to discover about how computers could enhance the quality of learning, the Government wished to see computers used not only to prepare students with vocational skills but also to enrich the whole curriculum:

> The Government recognizes the tremendous potential of IT as a classroom tool. Our policy is to promote IT in schools and see that it is used to raise educational standards. Our goal is ambitious: it is nothing less than the full integration of IT into all classroom studies. We want to increase the extent and effectiveness of schools' use of IT for the enhancement of teaching and learning for pupils of all ages and abilities right across the curriculum. Not only do we want pupils to learn with IT; we also want them to learn about IT, to experience its power and be able to use it in a discerning way both at school and later in adult life.
>
> (John Butcher, Speech as Schools Minister, 12th July 1989)

Vision alone, of course, is not enough. There are practical issues like the acquisition of computers and the training of teachers. This began with the offer of a single computer at half price to every secondary school and a basic technical training for two teachers. It was followed by a decade of initiatives from the Departments of Education and Industry placing a succession of British-made computers and other related technology in schools and teacher training establishments. The Government also stimulated the British software industry by providing subsidies for educational software development and purchase. It set up a regional network of computer technology resource, training, and information centers (though later this became centralized) and, in the late 1980s, provided funds for teachers already familiar with the technology to be withdrawn from schools to act as a network of teacher advisors.

But all this was not enough. By the middle of the decade, the Government had become impatient with what it saw as the educational system's continued under-achievement; its inability to innovate and raise standards; its resilience to change in general and to technology in particular. Butcher's speech above, after all, was only a late admission of the Government's belief that technology was important: it was not only vital that children should be equipped to live and work in a technological age, the presence of computers in schools ought to stimulate change and raise educational standards. In 1985 the Government produced a discussion paper *Better Schools* (DES, 1985) which indicated the way ahead. This was followed by a further paper, *New Technology for Better Schools* (DES, 1987), indicating the role of information technology in this process:

> The central aim of the strategy is to harness the potential of information technology for enhancing the quality of teaching and learning across the curriculum. ... But there is still a long way to go if IT's potential is to be fully exploited. It is still not a part of the teaching repertoire which all teachers fully appreciate or feel comfortable with; and for many pupils, access to IT is by no means the commonplace activity which it needs to be if the greatest benefit is to be gained.

To carry the strategy forward, the Government argued that there needed to be hardware "sufficient to make ready and frequent access a reality for all pupils"; high quality curriculum material and supporting software to take full advantage of the new, more powerful machines becoming available; in-service training; a cohort of advisory teachers to coordinate and lead the promotion of IT; a network for information and advice both between central government and local government and between local education authorities in hardware; and technicians—in order to free teachers from technical tasks "for which few will be well equipped and to allow them to concentrate on developing the pedagogical applications of the technology." Local education authorities were required to submit to the Secretary of State a statement of development policy for the coming five years. Among the issues which the development policy had to address were:

- the current pattern of provision between schools;
- the Authority's policy on the use of IT across the curriculum;
- policy and plans for support services for IT in schools;
- the management structure which the Authority proposed to adopt for the cohort of advisory teachers it was to set up;
- policy on cooperation with other local education authorities and teacher training institutions;
- policy on relevant industrial contributions and the framework for eliciting these; and
- a statement of the Authority's plans to bring together the range of relevant sources of finance—a succession of Government offers, contributions from industry, etc., in the context of a coherent schools IT policy for the Authority's area.

Quite naturally, local education authority chief education officers then turned to schools and demanded the same from them. But this was only an indication of what was to come.

## Development of a National IT Curriculum

In the following year, the Government decided to deal with schools directly and to legislate for change. The Education Reform Act of 1988 made technological innovation imperative in English schools. It resulted in a compulsory National Curriculum for all state schools in England and Wales. (Scotland and Northern Ireland have separate educational systems.) Statutory Orders were produced for each subject in the curriculum defining the program of study to be delivered. Each Order also contained attainment targets for the subject, and there was provision for national testing at the ages of 7, 11, 14, and 16 to see which levels of attainment pupils had achieved.

Within the National Curriculum, information technology is presented as a subject of study in its own right and all pupils now have a statutory right to "information technology capability." Pupils should be able to use information technology to communicate and handle information; design, develop, explore, and evaluate models of real or imaginary situations; and to measure and control physical variables and movement. They should be able to make informed judgments about the application and importance of information technology and its effect on the quality of life (DES, 1990). The Order for Technology contains a complete program of study for information technology together with 10 levels of attainment. It is worth giving some examples to demonstrate the technological extent of what teachers must now be prepared to teach and children to learn.

Within the first two years of schooling, all children should be taught that information technology can be used to help plan and organize ideas in written and graphical form; how to give instructions to electronic devices; and how to store, select, and analyze information using software. By the final two years of compulsory schooling, children should be taught to work together using discussion, explanation, and negotiation to improve the quality of the information presented via information technology; to use information technology to improve efficiency and to support new ways of working; to select software appropriate for a particular task or application; to design and implement an information technology-based system for use by others; to review and discuss their use of information technology and to consider applications in the outside world; and the impact on daily life, including environmental, ethical, moral, and social issues. In addition, more able students will be taught to define the information required, the purposes for which it is needed, and how it will be analyzed, and to take these into account in designing ways of collecting and organizing the information in a database; to analyze systems to be modelled using information technology, make choices in designing, implementing and testing them, and justify the methods they have used.

The significant point here is that information technology is not to be taught as a discrete subject. Pupils should acquire information technology capability through their study of other subjects and so all teachers are potentially participants in this innovation:

> ... our aim is to ensure that all pupils have a firm foundation of general information technology skills which can be developed through their work in subjects across the curriculum ...          (DES, 1989a, para 3.9)

In all subjects, information technology features within the individual programs of study and the attainment targets. For example, in the *Order for English* (DES, 1989b), children between the ages of 5 and 7 should be faced with reading material which reflects the real world—explicitly this should include computer printout and visual display. They should be able to produce copies of work drafted on a computer, and be encouraged to incorporate the printout in other work, including displays. In *History* (DES, 1991), pupils should have opportunities to use a range of historical sources, including computer based materials. It is suggested they use a database in learning how to ask questions, to select and organize historical information, and to use desktop publishing to present their results. In the learning and using of a modern foreign language, pupils should have regular opportunities to use computers. The program of study (NCC, 1991b) suggests language games, problem-solving, information retrieval, word processing, desktop publishing, and communicating via electronic mail.

## Implementation Plans

The statutory requirement for schools to incorporate information technology into the compulsory subjects of the National Curriculum generates a number of complex management issues. It challenges the former practice of schools where information technology was nonexistent or where the teaching of information technology was organized as a separate subject and justified in the traditional way as a preparation for pupils who will be living in a technologically rich society. But the greatest challenge is posed by the potential contribution that information technology can make to enhancing and enriching the quality of teaching and learning. To help schools achieve such a demanding technology curriculum, the Government, through its National Curriculum Council, has issued guidance to schools (NCC, 1990) to implement and sustain the innovation.

The guidance stresses that every school should have an information technology policy and a plan for its implementation. Schools, the guidance says, will wish to set short term goals (one to two years ahead) and long term aims (five years ahead). The policy will provide a framework for development and should among other things:

- provide a statement of intent for teachers, governors, and the local education authority;
- specify the principles for selecting, funding, and acquiring hardware and software;
- address resource availability, access, safety, and maintenance;
- specify plans for replacing equipment; and
- describe how the policy will be monitored and reviewed.

The implementation plan should:

- give guidance on the classroom organization of information technology, identifying appropriate teaching methods, hardware, and software;
- identify the contribution of each subject to the development of information technology capability;
- provide for coordination across the curriculum and age range;
- provide for rigor and progression, and for pupils to achieve their potential; and
- identify and address in-service training needs.

In preparing their information technology policy and implementation plan, schools should consider a variety of questions, such as the following:

- How should information technology across the curriculum be organized?
- Do our resources support our curriculum objectives?
- How can we organize the acquisition and allocation of resources?
- How can we improve our deployment of resources?
- What obstacles are impeding progress?
- How can we overcome these obstacles?
- How can we promote each teacher's practical competence?
- What external agencies (such as advisory teachers, computer education centers, and national associations) can we draw on for support and advice?

## IT Coordinators

The guidance goes on to discuss management responsibilities. Headteacher, middle management, and classroom teachers all have a role to play. The headteacher is to be responsible for ensuring that there is an information technology policy and that it is implemented. In some small schools, it suggests, all teachers may have a responsibility for decisions and planning with the headteacher retaining the coordinating role. In most schools, however, particularly in larger schools, it is recommended that there should be an information technology coordinator. The role of coordinator (especially in the secondary school) is a fairly recent organizational phenomenon which has emerged as a result of trying to find the means of managing curricular initiatives that extend across traditional subject boundaries (North, 1990). It is recommended that the coordinator should be assisted by a coordinating group for information technology, perhaps involving a member of the senior management team and two or three staff representatives of different subjects. The group should meet regularly to consider the school's information technology policy and implementation plan and to review practice.

The coordinator has a considerable number of duties related to the implementation of information technology in the curriculum. As all of those already engaged in the promotion of cross-curricular information technology know only too well (North, 1990), the associated management tasks are complex. For example, the National Curriculum Council specifies the following as some of the coordinator's responsibilities. (The tasks will vary slightly between primary and secondary schools.)

*Coordination*
- coordinating the writing of the school information technology policy;
- ensuring that the policy is implemented consistently throughout the school;

- establishing collaboration between year groups or across subject departments;
- assisting heads of department to produce their own information technology policy (at secondary level);
- ensuring that the program of study for information technology capability is covered by schemes of work;
- ensuring assessment and recording of each pupil's information technology capability.

*Resources*
- organizing resources to support the information technology policy and its priorities;
- ensuring safety of equipment;
- coordinating the identification of future needs;
- purchasing and maintenance of equipment;
- providing support for the evaluation of hardware and software.

*Staff Development and Support*
- assisting teachers to incorporate information technology;
- liaising with staff to identify training needs;
- coordinating the provision of in-service training;
- distributing information about applications, teaching strategies, and appropriate software and hardware.

*Monitoring and Review*
- coordinating the monitoring and review of information technology practice and provision;
- coordinating the review of information technology practice and provision;
- advising senior staff about the progress of the information technology policy.

*External Liaison*
- keeping up to date on technology developments and their use in the curriculum;
- liaising with other schools and advisory agencies.

## The Role of Teachers

While many innovation attempts have been thwarted by a failure to address management issues, this has not been wholly the case in England. The Government has not only attempted to present a vision of the place of information technology in English schools, it has also attempted to lead schools towards successful implementations of that vision through the creation of a management infrastructure capable of devising policy and implementation plans, articulating realistic goals, attending to resource provision, staff training and support, monitoring practice, and reviewing strategy. But while the Government may have attempted to attend to many of the necessary requirements for effective innovation, its strategy must, as must that of any leader in innovation, be supported by the articulation of a shared system of values and beliefs or the development of a new one (Schein, 1985; Sergiovanni & Corbally, 1984).

This innovation is essentially a top-down imposition on the vast majority of teachers. Many teachers have yet to be convinced of the Government's view of the place of information technology in education. It must be remembered that arguments in favor of introducing computers in schools formed part of a larger debate about the role of schooling in England. Many English teachers would not accept that schools have failed to meet society's needs, particularly the needs of industry, and they resent and are suspicious of the need for the forceful imposition of a National Curriculum upon them—even though some of it they might accept as good practice. While most teachers would probably appreciate the need for contemporary students to have some information technology familiarization and skill, they would not see that as being their duty unless they were Computer Studies teachers. Nor would they accept that information technology could enhance their own teaching—they do not see technology as the best answer to a problem; sometimes they don't even see the problem!

To some extent, teacher objections could have been (and were) allayed by the process the Government initiated to determine the new curriculum. It set up a working party in each subject area to advise on the rationale and content of the subject and presented the working party reports to the profession for consultation. In many instances, the expansive reports from these working parties provide excellent encapsulations of what many teachers would consider the best of good teaching practice. But they are markedly different from the stark curriculum Orders later laid before Parliament. Those statutory Orders were based upon the working party reports but excluded their underpinning philosophy. They contained programs of study to be taught and statements of what pupils should attain—not the reasons for teaching such programs nor for setting such attainments.

Already there have been revisions by the Secretary of State to these Orders, taking them further away from the original beliefs articulated by the working parties. As further revisions are introduced, or simply as we progress in time away from the publication of the original working party reports, teachers are less and less able to see the vision behind what they are instructed to do. It will be particularly difficult for new entrants to the profession who have not experienced the original drafting and consultation period of the curriculum to perceive let alone empathize with those aims. It is therefore important to note that the suggested school management of information technology within the National Curriculum does allow for the creation of teacher ownership of information technology policy. Each school must devise its own policy and implementation plan. While this may not exclude the government imposed framework, schools are free to extend beyond that framework and even within it there may still be scope for participation in building shared values and beliefs sustained with agreed social and technical support structures.

## Leadership from IT Coordinators

While there has been much attention to many aspects of the management of information technology innovation in schools since the curriculum was laid before Parliament, it is only recently that the real importance of leadership has gained prominence. For the information technology curriculum to work, much depends on the caliber of the coordinator. On the one hand, the coordinator must speak with conviction about what is required within the National Curriculum. The coordinator must have a vision not only of what is demanded by the Government but of what is possible within and beyond what the Government's dictates. The coordinator must believe that technology is capable of producing desirable change and identify what that change should be and how to go about it. The agenda appears in the National Curriculum guidance but its context, specific content, and purpose require vision from the coordinator. On the other hand, the coordinator needs to hear what the teachers believe themselves both positively and negatively about computers and then to move on to negotiate a culture which teachers can believe in and act upon. As the National Curriculum Council Guidance states: strong interpersonal skills, the skills to work with other teachers, and a good understanding of the curriculum are more important than strong technical skills (NCC, 1990). As a result, it would be a mistake to think of the most experienced user of computers on the staff as necessarily the best person to fill all the roles of the information technology coordinator.

> At any one time or, indeed, at the same time, the coordinator may be called upon to play the role of facilitator, in service trainer, consultant, planner, technician, curriculum designer, policy formulator, assessor, moderator, ego stroker, a hand holding nurse, and so on. They are also frequently expected to be able to adopt with ease a number of different personalities, moving from one situation where they are assertive to another where they are passive, from being protective of a teacher's shortcomings to pushing them in at the deep-end. At times they will feel that they can act with the status and authority of a knowledgeable expert, usually when talking about hardware or demonstrating the magic of a piece of software. At other times they might feel they lack the status and authority for a particular task, particularly when dealing with an uncooperative head of department on a higher grade allowance. (North, 1990, p. 39)

Some early enthusiasts certainly possessed several important qualities required of information technology coordinators: they were motivated and confident; they were obviously able to present convincing arguments to senior managers within schools and to potential hardware sponsors; they were also able to identify immediate uses of the technology in the curriculum. But they were often as interested in programming and bits and bytes as they were in the educational potential of the technology. They sometimes lacked greater vision and the ability to let others share it or participate in its construction. Leadership qualities, especially a sense of vision and a sensitive approach to dealing with colleagues, are far more important than technical expertise.

## IT Leadership from Administrators

Much of what has been said of the information technology coordinator also applies to the senior management in school. Her Majesty's Inspectors of Schools advise that: "often the day-to-day leadership in this field is devolved to a member of staff [but] ... involvement and commitment on the part of the headteacher are critical to the development of IT" (HMI, 1989). Recent documents from the National Curriculum Council have also emphasized leadership at senior management level:

> Senior management has an important role in supporting these [information technology] developments through providing its own leadership and a clear policy for the whole school:

> David Scott, head teacher at Calder High School: "As head teacher, I have to enthuse, I have to encourage and I have to support, making sure there is enough IT hardware and software for pupils and teachers to use and making sure that we have a clear view, as a school, as to where IT fits within our curriculum and what we want both of our teachers and of our pupils."
>
> (NCC, 1991a, p. 22)

Of course, the way that information technology is utilized in each subject will vary, and it is important for subject coordinators or Heads of Department to show strong leadership here. The National Curriculum Council's guidance prompts the Head of Department to consider how information technology can be used to enhance the teaching of the subject, taking account of the information technology requirements associated with the particular subject National Curriculum Order. At the same time, it is important for Heads of Department to identify which components of information technology capability from the Technology Order can be developed within the subject. The National Curriculum Council Guidance stresses that the Head of Department must help classroom teachers realize technological potential—identifying hardware and software and how it is to be used; enabling staff to exchange ideas for using information technology—through staff workshops, team teaching, sharing worksheets, and other resources; identifying staff needs for in-service training and involving all staff in the department in reviewing the use of information technology.

That last point—the involvement of all staff—was one advocated strongly by Her Majesty's Inspectorate of Schools. The Inspectorate suggests that once an agreed plan of action has been adopted, every teacher—not just the head or 'IT expert'—should contribute to its implementation and periodic review (HMI, 1989). The National Curriculum Council Guidance suggests that in primary schools teachers have shared responsibility for information technology and there may not therefore be a need for an information technology coordinator. All staff take responsibility for decisions and planning with the headteacher retaining the coordinating role. Shared leadership is therefore important. Even at secondary level, there is still scope for shared leadership if there is seen to be collective responsibility for the information technology policy and its implementation.

## IT Leadership from Teachers

Individual classroom teachers also have other opportunities to exhibit leadership and it is important to encourage them to do so when implementing technological change in schools. From the very first days of computers in schools, teachers have informally accepted responsibility for encouraging and supporting other teachers and student teachers in their use of technology. Such leadership can be driven by genuine conviction and first-hand experience. But the teacher can manifest some of those undesirable traits (referred to above) which easily make the computer buff unsuitable to be information technology coordinator. This kind of leadership can be very idiosyncratic and limited by the particular interests of the individual involved. This was especially the case among some early pioneers—particularly before a wider context and vision were urged upon them by the National Curriculum.

In England, practicing classroom teachers will now need to manifest individual leadership more than ever before. In 1992, the Government decided to increase the amount of school-based teacher training to sixty-six percent. Practicing teachers are now expected to take on board the major share of teacher training and this is no less true in technology than in any other subject. Indeed, in 1989, the Government issued demanding specifications for all teacher training courses in England. It required that:

> ... all courses should contain compulsory and clearly identifiable elements which enable students to make effective use of information technology (IT) in the classroom and provide a sound basis for their subsequent development in this field. They should be trained to be able to:
>
> (1) make confident use of a range of software packages and information technology devices appropriate to their subject specialism and age range;

(2) review critically the relevance of software packages and information technology devices appropriate to their subject specialism and age range and judge the potential value of these in the classroom;

(3) make constructive use of information technology in their teaching and in particular prepare and put into effect schemes of work incorporating appropriate uses of information technology;

(4) evaluate the ways in which the use of information technology changes the nature of teaching and learning.                    (DES, 1989d, para 6.6)

Since technology is to be used across the curriculum, it is reasonable to expect that classroom teachers of all subjects have a role to play here in helping student teachers achieve these goals. Admittedly, the move towards school-based teacher training has been accompanied by a revision of these demanding requirements, but it is important to remember that they were first articulated by a Government appointed committee of inquiry and were seen to be "a minimum aim" (DES, 1989c). It is currently thought that the final specifications for teacher training courses will contain similar aims—at least as recommendations if not as imperatives. A recent document produced  by the National Council for Educational Technology *et al.* (NCET, 1992), for example, maintains that students should still acquire a holistic understanding of the ways in which information technology contributes to teaching and learning together with an understanding of the developing nature of information technology capability and an awareness that it is integral to the whole structure and purposes of the National Curriculum. Practicing teachers should continue to develop these competences: adapting to curricular changes, to learners' needs, and to emerging technologies; maintaining a holistic understanding of information technology in the curriculum; and continuing to implement and evaluate information technology supported learning activities.

As they work together towards such goals, both practicing teachers and student teachers will be developing important aspects of technology leadership. The critical awareness demanded by the training criteria in relation to the relevance of software and hardware and the ways in which the use of information technology can change the nature of teaching and learning are vital attributes. Similarly, as teachers come to offer in all subjects the full technology program of study as specified within the National Curriculum, they must again develop skills to focus critically on the technology. In order to offer children a full information technology entitlement, it is specified within the National Curriculum that teachers must enable pupils to stand back from technology and evaluate its impact on themselves, other individuals, organizations and society while discussing the ethical, moral, and social issues raised.

## Conclusion

In English schools we should therefore be moving towards a culture in which it is acknowledged that teachers at all levels can help to lead technological innovation. The full benefits of information technology for education will be realized only when teachers, at all levels and in every subject have a clear and critical understanding of what information technology can offer them and the capability to make effective use of it (NCC, 1990, p. 21). Classroom teachers must quickly acquire not just a confidence in the technology and an ability to use it but also an understanding of the strengths and limitations of technology and of the attendant conceptual issues. Such understanding will appear explicitly in the content of their teaching; it will also inform their professional judgments. It will be demonstrable in the training of new recruits and in negotiation with and support of colleagues. The responsibility then falls to senior and middle managers to recognize and utilize these attributes of leadership where they exist and to foster them where they do not. All teachers ought to be in a position to make informed statements about technology, to see how it can be used to solve real problems in schools, and to put the technology to use with good effect.

Educational technology leadership ought to exist at all levels in schools. There is certainly scope for this if not a necessity within current Government initiatives. But while the Government may have forced its own technological agenda on schools, this is no reason why schools, with good leadership, should not and will not determine an agenda for themselves. Indeed, unless they do so, teachers may never come fully to see the technological and other demands which exist and the technological solutions which are available. The current National Curriculum technological innovation will then be in jeopardy. Far worse, the use of technology per se may predictably deteriorate into superfluous symbolic action enforced by external pressures and devoid of any inherent educational value or real school need espoused by teachers.

## References

Cory, S. (1990). Can your district become an instructional technology leader? *The School Administrator (Special Issue on Technology)*, 17–19.

Department of Education and Science [DES] (1985). *Better Schools*. London: Her Majesty's Stationery Office.

Department of Education and Science [DES] (1987). *New Technology for Better Schools*. London: Her Majesty's Stationery Office.

Department of Education and Science [DES] (1989a). *Design and Technology for Ages 5 to 16*. London: Her Majesty's Stationery Office.

Department of Education and Science [DES] (1989b). *English in the National Curriculum.* London: Her Majesty's Stationery Office.

Department of Education and Science [DES] (1989c). *Information Technology in Initial Teacher Training: Report of the IT in ITT Expert Group.* London: Her Majesty's Stationery Office.

Department of Education and Science [DES] (1989d). *Initial Teacher Training: Approval of Courses (Circular 24/89).* London: Department of Education and Science.

Department of Education and Science [DES] (1990). *Technology in the National Curriculum.* London: Her Majesty's Stationery Office.

Department of Education and Science [DES] (1991). *History in the National Curriculum.* London: Her Majesty's Stationery Office.

Fothergill, R. (1988). *Implications of New Technology for the School Curriculum.* London: Kogan Page.

Her Majesty's Inspectorate [HMI] (1989). *Information Technology from 5 to 16: Curriculum Matters 15.* London: Her Majesty's Stationery Office.

National Council for Educational Technology [NCET] (1992). *Competences in Information Technology.* Coventry: NCET.

National Curriculum Council [NCC] (1990). *Non Statutory Guidance: Information Technology Capability.* York: National Curriculum Council.

National Curriculum Council [NCC] (1991a). *Information Technology in the National Curriculum: Key Stages 1 to 4: Teachers' Notes.* York: National Curriculum Council.

National Curriculum Council (1991b). *Modern Foreign Languages: Consultation Report.* York: National Curriculum Council.

North, R. (1990). *Managing Information Technology: The Role of the IT Coordinator.* Londonderry: University of Ulster.

Schein, E. H. (1985). *Organizational Culture and Leadership.* San Francisco: Jossey-Bass.

Sergiovanni, T. J. & Corbally, J. E. (1984). *Leadership and Organizational Culture.* Chicago: University of Chicago Press.

## About the Author

*Brent Robinson* is The University Lecturer in Information Technology in Education and Fellow of Hughes Hall at the University of Cambridge. He was formerly a secondary school teacher and now develops in-service and degree courses for teachers in the management of technology. He is also currently the editor of the *Journal of Information Technology for Teacher Education.*

# Part III: Strategies

The three chapters in this final section present strategies for improving the quality, effectiveness or impact of educational leadership through technology. While each of these strategies focus on different aspects of educational technology, they all agree that current approaches to leadership training are not adequate for the future.

In Chapter 10, Withrow addresses the nature of educational leadership in an information rich society. He discusses the significance of ubiquitous telecommunications opportunities on learning and teaching, staff development of teachers and school administrators, and the educational infrastructure. Withrow argues that emerging telecommunications technology will fundamentally change education and hence its leadership.

Romiszowski and Criticos, in Chapter 11, make the case for an open learning philosophy for the training of educational technologists. An open learning philosophy refers to the planning and delivery of education which involves the learner as a collaborator in the process and is sensitive to individual needs, interests, and abilities. In the opinion of these authors, the current approach to preparing educational technologists does not respond to the real problems in schools and the workplace.

Chapter 12 is a call for a major restructuring of the education system with technology playing a major role in this overhaul. Perelman states that the problem is not simply spending more money on education, but improved productivity, especially in terms of technology leverage. He also insists that much more must be spent on education R&D and proposes the creation of a National Institute for Learning Technology.

Whether you agree or disagree with the suggestions made in these chapters, it is important to experiment with new strategies for leadership in educational technology. Almost everyone believes that our current education system is far from satisfactory—to change this situation we need better leadership. Hopefully, the ideas presented in this section (and in the previous chapters) provide some places to begin.

# 10/ Educational Leadership in an Information-Rich Society

## Frank B. Withrow

### Council of Chief State School Officers

*This chapter discusses the nature of educational leadership in an information-rich society. It examines the impact of ubiquitous telecommunication opportunities on: learning and teaching, staff development for teachers, staff development for administrators, and the educational infrastructure.*

## Introduction

If we examine the average high school graduate for the year 2000 and compare him or her with graduates of the year 1900, we will find some interesting differences. The world population had reached 1 billion by the year 1900. By the year 2000 the world population will reach 6 billion people. In affluent societies, such as the United States of America, the average 18-year-old will have spent much of his or her time doing things that were impossible and unheard of in 1900.

Most of the scientists that have lived during the history of mankind are alive today. Any citizen in an information-rich country has the possibility of having a library that only the rich could afford a few years ago. Encyclopedias on CD-ROM give a rapid and complete indexing of the articles in them. They allow the users to transfer quotations into a computer's word processing system. The telecommunication systems of the world offer users a cornucopia of resources that were once available to only the very few. Mass media provide an ocean of information that is available to all elements of a society.

The average 18-year-old will have listened to thousands of hours of recorded music and viewed thousands of hours of television by the time he or she graduates from high school. The average 18-year-old has access to automobile and air travel. Many will have traveled beyond the boundaries of their home community, state, nation, and continent. Through the network of worldwide telecommunications many students will have known and interacted with people in other parts of the world through direct voice links, computers, and one-way and two-way video communications.

From an information standpoint it is the best of times and the worst of times. Those who become sophisticated in the uses and manipulation of the communication and computing resources of the community will become the symbolic workers of society. They will have untold power at their finger tips, and through high performance computing and communication systems will work with others around the world. Those who fail to understand and learn to use the communications and computing resources will become an underclass totally disadvantaged in an increasingly competitive world.

Traditional western educational models have not changed since the early 1700s. Great lip service has been given to new educational models, but the fact remains that schools around the world are still patterned after the design of the early industrial age. Prior to the 1700s, knowledge in books was available only through scribes and scholars who served as gate keepers. With the widespread use of the printing press, libraries, and books became available to the masses. Cheap paper and printing presses democratized the knowledge base of society.

Our current educational system evolved from this expanded availability of books. It has served the world reasonably well until now. Within this century knowledge has exploded. This increase in knowledge has created two major influences on the world of education. First, the knowledge base is so large today that no single person or single system can possible define it. Second, the knowledge base is expanding at such a rapid rate that even the Library of Congress has difficulty cataloging and storing it. In the United States alone there are more than 50,000 books published annually. In business and government this year more than 3 trillion pages of information will be created. In an era that we predicted would be the age of the paperless office, our communication systems have accelerated the rate of creation of paper.

Raymond Kurzweil, writing in *Library Journal*, has questioned whether ink on paper is the best way to store and retrieve printed materials. He is acutely aware of the large installed base of print materials, but believes that we will ultimately use computer based electronic storage and retrieval systems. Already electronic encyclopedias are available and more accessible to the user than the more awkward paper and leather bound encyclopedias of yesterday.

President George Bush, working with the State Governors, called for a set of National Educational Goals. This represented another attempt to establish national educational policy. The principle of universal rights to a public education was a national policy established early in the history of the nation. The current call to meet the National Goals by the year 2000 can be just as significant as universal public education. Jack Bowsher, former director of IBM education, warns us that changes in policy do not always guarantee reform. Bowsher believes there are four stages of true reform. First is problem identification, second is the creation of a vision, third is change agent  empowerment with authority to make the change, and fourth is believers capable of implementing the change.

Former Secretary of Education Lamar Alexander's AMERICA 2000 plan, which exemplified the invention of a new American school, met Bowsher's first condition. What is needed is the leadership to create the vision of what that system will be. There are efforts that may in fact create the foundations for that new dream of what American schools can be. The next few years will determine whether we will begin to meet the challenge or whether we are willing to do business as usual. A major and compelling question is what role will technology play in the reform movement. Every magazine article, newspaper story, or television program about education reform depicts attractive children either at computers or with computers and television in the background of their classrooms. However, when we examine the installed base of computers and other technologies in schools, it is characterized by the following factors:

- Most classrooms do not even have a common telephone.
- Most computers in use are obsolete and lack the power of first class computers.
- Only a handful of schools are equipped with distance learning resources.
- Few teachers and administrators have been trained in the use of modern telecommunication resources.
- Technology has not been institutionalized.
- These services are the first to go under the budget axe in tight fiscal budgets.
- Many schools are without enough textbooks, pencils, and paper.

Technology in general is more prevalent in the homes of the students than in their classrooms. There are 35 million Nintendo machines in American homes; 85% of families with school-aged children have VCRs; 15% of American homes have computers; almost 100% have radios, televisions, and telephones. While there are some examples of the uses of these home based technologies by the schools, there is neither the understanding nor the commitment by educational leaders who understand the importance of such technology.

The economies of scale of the educational technologies demands national and regional programs. Educational leadership must understand the importance of these resources and design programs that assure they will be implemented in the classroom and in the homes of our students.

Every citizen in a modern information-rich society must be able to use the symbolic mediums of his or her society effectively. Each person must originate, transmit, and receive information. Information becomes knowledge when the user translates it into meaningful social interactions. In short, we need a new "bill of rights" for every learner in a telecommunications-rich world (see Table 1).

 Table 1

---

*The Learner's Bill of Rights*
*In a Telecommunications Rich World*

*1. Every citizen is entitled to open access through public switched universal broadband telephone systems, cable television, and broadcast television to the information resources of our society.*

*2. Educational resources including libraries, schools, television, interactive multimedia, audio and person to person communications systems shall be equally accessible at affordable costs to all citizens in their homes, classrooms, and workplaces.*

*3. All public/private partnerships in telecommunications shall have reserved educational components available through high performance communications and computing systems.*

*4. Traditional public and private elementary and secondary schools, colleges, universities, distance learning providers, and libraries shall have access to the switched universal broadband systems at cost rates that are in the interest of the nation. Such rates may include Federal and State subsidies if required. At least thirty percent of telecommunications resources shall be reserved for educational uses.*

*5. The library community led by the Library of Congress shall create an electronic multimedia library of educational materials accessible by all learners in the nation.*

---

## Educational Reform in a Telecommunications-Rich World

Educators must be at the decision table when domestic telecommunications polices are set. Modern high performance communication and computing systems will have a major impact on the very nature of learning and teaching. The ideas presented here are intended to stimulate and focus the discussion about domestic telecommunications uses in education. For the purposes of this chapter we have divided the educational needs into the following categories:

- learning and teaching;
- staff development for teachers;
- staff development for administrators; and
- the telecommunications infrastructure.

### Learning and Teaching

The visions of learning and teaching in many reform proposals stress: the active involvement of the learner in the learning process; attention to intellectual and emotional skills at many levels; preparation of young people to assume responsibilities in a rapidly changing world of increasingly diverse cultural and political realities; and flexibility among students who will enter a world of work that will demand life-long learning. The Department of Labor estimates that most workers entering the work force today will change job skills at least five times in their work lives. The implications of this perspective of the learner's role include:

1. **Access to a broad range of learning resources.** Learners can no longer be limited to a single text or a series of texts, nor for that matter the limitations of most school libraries. Learners must have access to a variety of information resources including major libraries, computer databases, software programs, multimedia programs, content experts, and other up-to-date and comprehensive knowledge bases and communications systems.

2. **Active control of their learning resources.** Learners must be able to actively manipulate "raw data," must be able to put information together in many forms, must be able to create intellectual structures rather than simply respond to frameworks that others have designed. Learners must have the knowledge to use information tools and have access to them.

3. **Participation by learners in individualized learning experiences** based upon their skills, knowledge, interests, and goals. Individualized instruction does not mean isolated instruction, but instruction that is tailored to the specific needs of each student.

4. **Access to collaborative learning teams** that enable the learner to work with others to accomplish mutually determined goals critical to long-term personal growth, success, and satisfaction. Such activities shall not be limited to an individual class, school, or community. Through

telecommunications such projects may include students in other localities and schools.

5. **Experience in working on problem-solving tasks** that are relevant to the contemporary and future workplaces. Such experiences must be real and not make-work designed by others, but reflect the realities of the higher order thinking skills required in problem solving.

The teacher's role changes in an information-rich educational environment. The school and the teacher are no longer the sources of all knowledge, but act to coach learners to facilitate the use of the resources and tools they need to explore and create new knowledge and skills. For teachers this implies a number of changes from the agricultural/industrial model of schools. Teachers must be able to:

1. **Coach learners in the use of information and knowledge bases** as well as provide access for learners to use such resources.

2. **Support learners as they become active** in the self-directed learning process indicated above.

3. **Assess and manage the learning environment** in which learners are using information resources. They must be able to coach learners in the development of collaborative experiences; monitor student progress; provide editorial support feedback on student work; and offer real opportunities for the publication of student work.

4. **Assess student work** that is consistent with the philosophy of the learning strategies being employed and student performance.

### Staff Development for Teachers

Twenty-one percent of the current teaching staff in American schools are over 52 years old. This means that a new wave of teachers and supervisors will take their place in schools in this decade. This is as important a time in American education as the post World War II period, when a new generation of teachers, supervisors, and administrators set the model of our current system. While it will be a time of change, it will also be a time for creativity and new educational programs. The telecommunication tools that will be available to educators means a new basic concept of what education should be. With this change there will come a new role for the teacher based upon new models of learning and teaching. As a result teachers in their professional preparation and throughout their careers will be required to be sophisticated users of information resources. Teachers must be prepared to perform:

1. **The role of the teacher as a coach and resource facilitator** that nurtures active learners who participate in their own learning processes.

2. **The management of a wide range of communication and information tools** that are currently available and will be increasingly available in the future. These tools will facilitate active learning involvement by students.

3. **Professional interactions with other teachers and content specialists** within their community and across the nation. Teachers must be able to exchange ideas and knowledge through broadband telecommunications. Teachers need to understand their intellectual and professional environments in terms of their community, their states, their region, their nation, and indeed the global community.

4. **With the support services of professional guides and aides** that enable them to fully participate as professionals. Teachers are the essential front line professional in any educational system. Their knowledge and skills are essential to the well-being of any program; therefore, they must have the libraries and technical resources that enable them to fulfill their responsibilities. Yet, today, few schools purchase any new professional books for faculty, and professional libraries are very rare in school buildings.

### Staff Development for Administrators

School administrators require an integral understanding of the impact of technology on the management and operation of schools. The central office has often been cited as a cause for rising costs of education. Most school systems have not taken advantage of modern management tools based upon cost-accounting for elements of the program.

If, for example, many administrators are asked to justify the capital outlay for interactive multimedia programs, they do not have the tools to do it. Moreover, we constantly hear of computers that were bought ten years ago and now gather dust. Those tools may have more than paid for their costs, but have become obsolete. Schools in general have not developed systems for inventorying obsolete equipment and amortizing it, nor even understanding the information needed to make such judgments.

Administrators need to develop skills that will:

1. **Enable them to respond effectively to calls for accountability.** Accountability requires effective and efficient performance of the school, district, or broader system for which the administrator is responsible. It also requires the development of effective means for systematically gathering, analyzing, and reporting information pertaining to the accountability measures required.

2. **Enable them to find ways to forge new collaborative relations** among schools, businesses, social service agencies, and other providers that may be of importance to the school's teaching and learning missions.

3. **Enable them to share information and resources** with other schools. Enable them to enter into state and regional compacts that can create regional information databases, electronic libraries, and telecommunications services.

4. **Enable them to meet assessment goals** through the sharing of regional and national measurement and assessment systems, and to participate in the development of assessment systems on regional and national levels.

5. **Enable them to have access to management information** systems that can assure effective and efficient operation of the learning and teaching resources that are their responsibilities. Administrators, just as teachers, must have the tools that allow them to function in an information-rich world.

**The Telecommunications Infrastructure**

When possible the educator should use the public systems of domestic telecommunications facilities that are available. The private/public telecommunications infrastructure has the advantage of economies of scale in providing services. Consequently, the costs can be spread over the more efficiently operating system. It is assumed that there are costs and that education should pay a reasonable share of such costs. However, if the nation determines that domestic telecommunications resources are an essential part of lifelong education, then public decisions can be made to provide reserved spectrums and subsidized prices.

The issue at this time is not cost but demonstration of the impact such systems can have on the revitalization and design of the new American school. High powered communication and computing networks, such as, the National Research and Education Network (NREN) are concepts that must be demonstrated and applied to the learning and teaching processes at all school levels. The following education-based issues must be raised:

1. If learners, teachers, administrators, and others concerned with learning and teaching are to use telecommunications technologies, those technologies must be accessible. Lack of a telephone in a classroom becomes an insurmountable barrier to the use of electronic mail, hands-on computer science experiments, and other telecommunications uses. At the building level schools must be wired for telecommunications if they are to access telecommunications resources.

2. Capitalization of the hardware required for effective usage of telecommunications is an international issue. What is a fair share for each government jurisdiction? What is a fair share for the commercial telecommunications vendor? Who should own the hardware?

3. Is it enough to build the railroad? Who will provide the electronic libraries needed to feed a fully operational education telecommunications system? What will be the cost for the development of the curriculum strands? What is a reasonable cost for the use and delivery of the education resources through the telecommunications network? We have established in the broadcast field some fair-use rules, but these in fact do not cover the actual costs of development and delivery. Who will develop the software for the system? Who will store it and how will it be retrieved?

4. The ultimate desire is that technology becomes transparent from the users viewpoint ... that the technology is a servant of the education process and that systems are integrated into a user friendly resource.

5. A truly international system will allow for free and easy access to persons and resources throughout the world. The international educational telecommunications system should be as accessible as current direct dialing of long distance telephone calls. All citizens should have a right to access the system from their home, school, or workplace.

## About the Author

*Frank Withrow* is Director of Learning Technologies at the Council of Chief State School Officers and was formerly with the U.S. Department of Education, where he managed many major educational technology efforts including the "Star Schools," "Sesame Street," and "Voyage of the Mimi" programs. He obtained his Ph.D. from Washington University in St. Louis, Missouri.

# 11/ The Training and Development of Educational Technologists for the 21st Century

## Alexander J. Romiszowski

Syracuse University

## Costas Criticos

University of Natal

*This chapter argues for an open learning philosophy for the training of educational technologists, based upon a holistic interpretation of the systems approach. The current approach to preparing educational technologists does not respond to the deepening crisis in education and training around the world. It is necessary to adopt an open curriculum that minimizes the boundary between academia and the workplace and encourages collaboration among institutions.*

## Introduction

In this chapter, we examine to what extent the current practice of educational technology is attuned to the present and future needs and characteristics of education and training systems. We then follow by arguing for an open learning approach to the training and development of future educational technologists. But what is educational technology? And what is open learning? Indeed, the title of this chapter will almost inevitably conjure up a variety of images. The concepts that readers hold of educational technology may range from the mere presence and use of electronic media (particularly computers) in the classroom to the semantically more correct interpretation as the process of applying science to educational improvement. Similarly, open learning to some readers may signify a system or institution that utilizes broadcast telelectures and other distance teaching methods (as in Open University), but others will understand the term as a process of flexible planning and delivery of education which involves the learner as collaborator in this process and is thus sensitive to individual learner needs, interests, and capabilities.

While acknowledging this rich variety of interpretations, we shall in this chapter be using these two terms in their broader or process connotations. We start by examining some aspects and implications of this view of educational technology as an applied science. From this position, it is clear that educational technology is or at any rate should be intimately interested and enmeshed in issues of leadership. A discipline committed to advancing educational efficacy by systematic design, development, and evaluation of educational systems is, by definition, a leader in educational change. It offers the "tools" to make evaluative statements on the educational worth of current systems as well as to produce innovative systems that respond to educational problems and opportunities. However, as an evolving discipline, it too must adapt its approaches and extend its "toolbox" to adequately respond to new educational philosophies and theories. Otherwise, it is unlikely to fulfill its expected leadership role.

Over the last few years we have seen an increasing interest in critical perspectives of our field. Some of the landmarks of this growth are evidenced by the educational technology literature on constructivism, situated cognition, holistic perspectives, soft-system theory, feminist theory, and critical theory. According to Hlynka and Nelson (1991, p. iv) educational technology is in a crisis in which it has become "stuck fast in a technological, means-ends model." In their book, *Paradigms Regained*, they appeal for educational technology to move beyond the limits of one or two narrowly defined paradigms. The crisis according to them and others is due in part to educational technology's isolation and disinterest in the central debates in education that examine assumptions that underpin educational practice. These limitations—"the problem of objective knowledge"—are blamed for the undermining of the emancipatory conception of higher education (Barnett, 1990, p. 28).

As educational technology practitioners, we have a great deal of experience in evaluating and designing systems for clients and less experience of designing for ourselves. Syracuse University, like most North American universities (Elson, 1992), is facing a challenge to restructure its schools in the face of falling state and federal grants, a depressed economy, and falling student enrollment. We, like so many of our colleagues, face the ultimate challenge of evaluating our own systems and innovating for our own institutions and students. When we are part of the system under consideration, it is difficult to be our usual objective selves—we become reflective and doubtful of our own assumptions. The word "doubt" has never been part of the educational technologist's everyday language—our field is associated with confidence and optimism and a belief in the fundamental soundness of our theories. This is in marked contrast to the critical theorists who question taken-for-granted explanations and fundamental assumptions. This chapter attempts a critical examination of imperatives for training educational technologists in the twenty-first century.

## Leadership and Vision

The assumptions we have of education and knowledge—our epistemologies—manifest themselves as the key issues of leadership and vision. The discussion on epistemology is not a peripheral interest, but rather a central issue that impacts on the way we teach, learn, and view our role as educational technologists.

> .... the way we know has powerful implications for the way we live. Every epistemology tends to become an ethic, and every way of knowing tends to become a way of living. The relation established between the student and the subject, tends to become the relation of the living person to the world itself. Every mode of knowing contains its own moral trajectory, its own ethical direction and outcomes. (Palmer, 1990, p. 107)

An exploration of the different educational trajectories that characterize higher education yields two major orientations of *dissemination* and *development*—which are associated with Palmer's epistemologies of *objectivism* and *relatedness* (Palmer, 1990; Snell, Hodgson & Mann, 1987; Boot & Hodgson, 1987). In Table 1, Boot and Hodgson (1987) make explicit what these different orientations mean in higher education. This line of analysis is not to suggest that one orientation is better than the other or that only one vision is valid. If, as we have argued earlier, educational technology is enmeshed in issues of leadership, then we need to add that this leadership is bounded by the epistemologies, orientations, and visions of the leaders. A limited understanding and theoretical inflexibility will undoubtedly lead to leadership of a limited validity and utility. This can be illustrated by the type of "vision" that a bicycle rider has to exercise. The rider's *terminal* vision looks ahead and focuses on a particular objective, while the peripheral or *procedural* vision pays attention to the road condition and other vehicles. Failure to exercise both terminal and procedural vision will result in disaster—both a clear vision of the destination and an awareness of contextual factors of the journey are essential. These visions are not exclusive alternatives or sequential variants but operate simultaneously. Hylnka and Nelson (1991, p. 107) argue for a polyfocal vision in which all three of the main metaphors of educational technology—tools, systematic, and systemic—operate in a synergistic combination.

Table 1.
Two Orientations to Open Learning
(Adapted from Boot & Hodgson, 1987.)

|  | DISSEMINATION | DEVELOPMENT |
|---|---|---|
| **Assumptions about knowledge** | Knowledge as **valuable commodity** existing independently of people. Can be stored and transmitted. Epistemology of objectivism | Knowing as **process** of engaging with and attributing meaning to the world, including self in it. Epistemology of relatedness. |
| **Assumptions about learning** | **Acquisition and addition** of facts, concepts, and skills. | **Elaboration and change** of the meaning-making processes. Enhancement of personal competence. |
| **Purpose of education** | **Dissemination** of stored knowledge | **Development** of the whole person |
| **Meaning of independence** | **Individualization** | **Autonomy** |
| **Basis of learner choice** | **Cafeteria selection** from a set range of carefully prepared dishes | **Self catering** planning menus, deciding on raw materials required, and experimenting with ways of preparing dishes |

A similar challenge is set before educational technologists by Hawkridge (1991, p.106) in which he advocates "a mature and valid educational technology" which arises from the "dialectic between the operative and normative aspects of the field." Snell, Hodgson, and Mann (1987) see this maturity in relation to distance education as an evolution towards open learning. They repeat the appeal for maturity and synergy of the authors cited earlier so that educators do not simply locate themselves in the dissemination or development camp but move towards what they call "developmental dissemination."

In addition to the maturity gained through a dialectic advocated by Hawkridge, a careful and critical examination of our practice reveals ways in which valuable principles and ideas have been devalued and sterilized by a lack of procedural vision. A notable example of this devaluation is evident in the variable use and often misuse of the term "systems approach" when describing the processes and procedures actually implemented by educational technologists in their practical work. To many outside observers of educational technology or instructional design and development processes, the systems approach often appears to be a procedure of stages through which the work of a project should go in order for it to be easily managed and which is completely devoid of creativity and imagination. Indeed, this may be the case in many institutionalized settings where educational technology approaches have become used on a large scale and many often poorly trained personnel are recruited to do task analysis, curriculum planning, materials design and development, media production, and so on. Generally speaking, the larger and more business-like the organization, the more detailed and more lockstep the set of procedures that ultimately gets institutionalized under the title of educational technology, instructional design, or systems approach.

However, the term "systems approach" grew out of general systems theory and cybernetics, where it was coined to mean a very open-ended, creative, and heuristic approach to dealing with the understanding and improvement of complex, probabilistic systems, such as, among others, human organizations in general (Romiszowski, 1981). The science of cybernetics as the science of control of complex probabilistic systems grew up as an inter-disciplinary science seeking the commonalties between any area where complex, large, and probabilistic systems have to be in some way controlled or designed or put to work effectively (Ackoff, 1960; Pask, 1961). The systems approach was therefore originally a way of looking at a complex reality in the awareness that it was not completely controllable in a deterministic manner as many simpler mechanical systems might be (Romiszowski, 1970; Beer, 1959). From this realization came the basic principles of the systems approach which involve the careful analysis of interrelationships existing between interacting subsystems and the interpretation of these interactions in terms of predicting what may happen in other parts of the system if certain changes are made in a specific part (Neil, 1969). Another important principle, the cybernetic principle of control by feedback, grew out of the realization that complexity cannot be planned and implemented successfully the first time around, but that an iterative process of approximation to goals by trying a first so-called optimal or best attempt solution is followed by evaluating what worked and what didn't work (Neil, 1970).

The whole process is in fact heuristic rather than algorithmic, and creative rather than mechanistic and systematic. It has been convenient to describe the process as a set of phases or stages, but it is unfortunate that this description has often been presented in some form of flowchart that has then been interpreted by later generations as a directive algorithm to be slavishly followed and not in any way modified in the light of the real situation which is being dealt with. The realization of what a systems approach meant originally might suggest a number of ways in which the design and development of curricula for a rapidly changing society should be tackled in contrast to what appears to be the case in many projects carried out under the banner of educational technology and systems approach. The systems approach is principally a way of thinking (Emery, 1969), which enables one to have the vision necessary for effective leadership.

## Crisis in Higher Education

The need for a broad understanding of educational technology is perhaps no where more evident than in the structure and systems of higher education. A number of indicators show US higher education as inflexible and unable to respond to the rapidly changing educational terrain (Hart, 1992). Higher education faces major challenges in terms of both scale and complexity. Education and training is becoming the major US and international enterprise (Stonier, 1988). Education, now one of the biggest "business" activities, generates 2.7% or $100 Billion of the US Gross Domestic Product (Elson, 1992). The fourteen and a half million students in higher education represent an increasingly complex market—one that Hart (1992) says cannot be satisfied by the traditional universities.

The complexity is evident in these statistics: Forty percent of all higher education students are part-time students, and one third of all students are over twenty five years (Elson, 1992). Not only are more students registering as part-timers but the additional burden for both full-time and part-time students is the high unemployment rate. They are either workers or dependent on one or more workers whose income is in jeopardy. CNN news reports claim that in 1991, almost one in ten workers was unemployed and one in five was unemployed sometime during the year. If twenty percent of the US labor force was unemployed sometime during the year, this must surely result in increased instability and demands on working students. The image of the young, financially stable, and full-time student body is false.

A similar crisis situation can be discerned in the area of industrial training and human resource development. The American Society for Training and Development (ASTD) and the US Department of Labor recently concluded one of the most comprehensive studies of human resource development. They found evidence that the pedagogical crisis in higher education which was examined earlier is even more severely repeated in the industrial and corporate world. In spite of the shift in the economic center of gravity, from material to intellectual capital in the post-industrial era, US employers overall contribute only 1.4% of their payroll to training—well below ASTD and Department of Labor's recommended 4% (Carnevale & Schulz, 1990 ). The training is in addition not evenly distributed. Fifty percent of all training is undertaken in 15,000 or 0.5% of the 3.8 million companies. US companies have a much lower investment in training than their counterparts in the UK, where companies spend the equivalent of $1176 on each worker compared with the US average of $256 (Carnevale, 1991).

Industrialists and economists are realizing that profitability and worker earnings are directly related to training and especially formal on-the-job training. With studies which show workers with formal on-the-job training earnings as 25% higher than those who do not receive training, workers and management are realizing that "... learning is the rationing hand that distributes earnings in the American economy" (Carnevale, 1991).

Notwithstanding the undisputed value of industrial training for advancing company profits and worker income, ASTD and others charge that training programs are often inappropriate. Estimates made by some educational technologists who favor the performance technology approach suggest that maybe 70% or more of the training budget is poorly applied in either developing training that is not really necessary or omitting to create the conditions on the job for the newly trained personnel to actually apply what they have learned.

Another factor contributing to the training crisis is the newly developing high tech business environment of the 1990s. This has resulted in a move towards knowledge work and the associated rapid change in the details of the work that any individual person does. Whereas the "hot button" of the majority of companies of today and the last decade has been to deal with the problems of workplace illiteracy brought about by the general failure of the elementary and high school system to impart basic skills to a significant proportion of children, the battle cry for the next decade is going to be critical thinking skills, learning to learn, and trainee autonomy or trainee directedness in the planning of individual programs of self-development. An aging workforce and the attrition of skilled workers is an additional concern in the corporate and professional world. The American Library Association (ALA) reports that forty percent of their 197,000 members will be at least 65 years old by the year 2000. ALA has responded to this trend by establishing a council to develop "virtual classrooms" through distance education networks. Their commitment to support current professional staff and train new staff is being realized outside of the traditional university. While the ALA and others seek to recreate the classroom experience in a "virtual classroom" the time may have come for far more radical solutions that redefine rather than recreate the traditional classroom. Open learning, the most prominent theme in training for the 21st century, is one such redefinition in which clients (students and employers) exert influence and control over the curriculum and its modes of delivery.

## Opening the Curriculum

Open learning challenges the boundaries between academies as well as between academy and workplace to open the curriculum in ways welcomed by both student and employer. As a result of the increasing ease of transition to the workplace through linkages between academy and industry, the student develops a competency to learn in a varied and experiential manner, and the employer develops the competency to facilitate learning.

Barnett (1990) sees the professionalization of higher education curriculum as the biggest shift in the practice of higher education in the UK over the past 30 years. In the UK polytechnic and college system alone, at least one third of the students are engaged in some form of "professional placement" or internship as part of their degree program. No comparable figures were uncovered for the US, but a similar trend is noticeable. Most US degree programs now make provision for approximately 10–20% of the program credits to be earned by independent or field/internship experience. Special field experience or service learning departments in one form or another can be found on most campuses. In contrast to these general trends towards flexibility and opening out of the curriculum, instructional technology (IT) degree programs in the US have become increasingly closed. Johnson's (1992) survey of 168 US universities offering degrees in IT shows that only 7% offer independent study or self-instructional formats. Their rules are becoming increasingly rigid—there is gradual reduction in combined Master's degrees, and the number of universities that require continuous enrollment in the Master's degree has risen from 6% in 1984 to 11% in 1992.

Colleges and universities in the US are finding new ways of offering a wider choice of programs without increasing faculty. John Wood Community College (JWCC) does not duplicate what neighboring educational institutions offer, but rather contracts with them to offer services to JWCC students. Between 1974 and 1988, 30,000 students have participated in courses offered through the "educational common market." Now this has been expanded to include industrial settings in the common market consortium (Drea & Armistead, 1988). In our field, however, there are few examples of collaboration between educational technology programs. Interchange of faculty to teach a specialist course or two during the summer break or during a sabbatical year is typically the extent to which participants in one program might profit from another. The concept of encouraging and helping a student to construct a personalized program composed of course units from various institutions is still quite foreign to us. Even the use of distance education delivery methods, which would be one way of facilitating student access to a wider selection of course offerings (and incidentally a prominent topic in most of our curricula), is less practiced in the educational technology programs than in many others.

Collaborative arrangements in the US extend to many international locations through a variety of "programs abroad." In some cases these collaborations seek ways of incorporating international scholarship rather than mere exotic locations. An example of such an arrangement is the Master's degree in International Relations offered by the American University in Washington and the Ritseumeikan University in Kyoto, Japan. Students enroll in either country for their first year and then spend the second year in the other country (Elson, 1992). On a much bigger international scale, the Commonwealth Network for Cooperation in Distance Education is attempting to realize the world's most comprehensive educational network; they plan to "allow students anywhere in the commonwealth to take any course from any university in the commonwealth" (Daniel, 1988). The number of possible courses, available fully or partly through distance education, on an open-learning basis, adds up to many thousands (Romiszowski, 1991).

## Resources for Open Learning

In addition to structural changes essential for implementing open learning, teacher competencies and materials need to be consistent with the open learning philosophy. Networking and collaborative arrangements between universities, workplaces, and other educational institutions provide a contextual framework for opening the curriculum but attention must also be paid to the qualities of educational facilitators and materials at these sites.

Even well-established programs which have been based on principles of open learning have found these principles subverted by untrained open learning teachers who relied on approaches of the traditional university (Knapper, 1988). In a recent study of a distance education program (Wolcott, 1991), it was found that little or no attention was paid to student considerations or methodology. The teachers were preoccupied with "covering the content" in the "given time."

Finally, according to Bates (1990), we need to pay attention to both variants of interactivity, social and individual, both of which need to feature in education. It is possible, for instance, to have social interaction in a classroom or computer conferencing system without sufficient attention being paid to the personal or individual interactivity in which the learner wrestles with experience, and in which he or she constructs and personalizes knowledge. Educational planners need to be cautioned against a myopic concern with delivery and content, which excludes the possibility of allowing the student, community, and employer from writing themselves into the curriculum.

## A Rationale for an Open Learning Approach
## to Training Educational Technologists

If we take a systems view of an educational technologist both in training and development and later in professional practice, we could utilize the CIPP model (Stufflebeam *et al.*, 1971), popularized by its application to evaluation, to illustrate why the current approaches to the development of educational technologists may be part of the reason for distortions of the systems approach that we alluded to earlier in the chapter.

We will initiate this examination by considering the *Product* element of the CIPP model (Context, Input, Process, and Product). Our product is a technology, or at least that is what the name educational technology would tend to imply. A technology is different from a science in the sense that scientists seek to establish knowledge, and technologists seek to use knowledge for practical purposes. The essence of the training and development of an educational technologist should be to develop competencies in the successful solution of real-life complex problems. In this context, problem solving can both mean putting right something which is inadequate or wrong and also seizing an opportunity to be innovative. If we take this view, then we can paint a general picture of the types of product outcomes or objectives that ought to be measured at the end of a program of training and development of educational technologists. These objectives would be related to the evaluation of how well particular practical problems, whether of curriculum design and implementation or materials design and implementation, are actually tackled by our trainees. It is essential that at some point during the program of training, our educational technologists carry out a form of cognitive apprenticeship where they work in real-life contexts on real-life problems and are observed and evaluated to see what level of competence they have developed. This would imply that at least part of the training and development program should be real-life based, project-based, or on-the-job.

We now move on to the aspect of the *Process*. What sort of process would one expect to see in operation during the education and training of an educational technologist who is expected to be a successful real-life problem solver at the end of the day? We can look at the process aspect of the CIPP model from two viewpoints:

(1) the process as it is orchestrated by the teacher or the teaching system;
(2) the process as it goes on within the mind of the learner.

From the teaching system's point of view, the one overriding principle that has yet to be challenged is that the situations used for demonstration and for practice during training should bear a close resemblance to what is expected as post-training performance. This would therefore imply that much of the contents presented and the exercises or practice presented would again be related to the interpretation, analysis, and solution of complex real-life educational problems. Much of the methodology of presentation would be through use of case studies or through project work or through other methods that can be used to allow the learner to interact with a multi-faceted complex problem. Much of the teaching of the details that have to be pulled together in order to deal with this problem could be left for the learner to sort out by accessing books or electronic knowledge bases or other learners.

The second aspect of process, the part that goes on within the learner's mind, should be relevant to the development of skills required to deal with novelty and complexity. In learning heuristic skills, the emphasis is less on "practice makes perfect" and more on "practice *preceded and followed by analytical and evaluative reflection* makes perfect." The models suggested by Schon (1987) in his "reflective practitioner" approach may be an applicable basis for planning the learning process from the viewpoint of the learner. Essential ingredients for the realization of such a process in practice are a variety of complex, multi-faceted problems at different levels of difficulty and an opportunity to interact with others who may stimulate reflective processes by considering different viewpoints on the problems or, in the case of a tutor, taking the Socratic position of challenging the logical structure of the learner's deductions.

Moving on to the *Input* element in our systems model, this can be construed at the learning level as the content that will be presented to the learner to deal with. In the context of educational technology, this would be both the general theories and the specific principles of learning and teaching. Given that we've already postulated that the ideal training situation for our educational technologist is to be based in a real-life work or simulated work situation, then the content will spring from that work situation in terms of the problems that are presented. The general principles used already exist in fairly well specified knowledge structures and can be made available in either paper or electronic format as reference material for selective browsing and application to the problems that present themselves in reality. As educational technologists work in a number of different contexts ranging from job-related training to totally non-vocational education and across a whole range of different disciplinary content areas, the specific content of the problems to be solved is not something that would be predetermined in the curriculum as a set of situations common to all educational technology students. On the contrary, it would be the task of the individual student to collaborate with the training organization or the tutor to negotiate appropriate problem situations, which would be satisfactory both from the viewpoint of relevance to the reality in which the individual student works and also of appropriate complexity and challenge. We see here the role of open learning coming in as an essential element in the structuring of a curriculum so that it can be negotiable and adaptable to both the needs and the current skill levels of each individual participant.

Finally, we come to *Context* in the CIPP model. Here this implies the organizational or societal context within which the whole of educational technology and indeed the education process itself takes place. It is here that we realize that technique in the application of theoretical principles to the solution of a problem is not sufficient to guarantee the solution. This is especially important in the implementation and dissemination of that solution within the real-world context to people who are the so-called "stakeholders" and others who act as "gatekeepers," "reactionaries," or enthusiastic "early adopters." Experienced project managers in the business world commonly claim that "success is 20% technique and 80% tactics." By "technique" they mean all that can be learned in the formal study of principles applied to particular problems, and "tactics" is what is learned in the "university of life" by learning what can in fact be implemented in a particular context without fear of rejection. In a heart transplant operation, success is determined more by how the organism as a whole is treated in order to promote its acceptance of the newly implanted organ than by the surgical skills of implanting the organ itself. So also in organizational systems, there is more skill and know-how involved in priming the macro system or context so that it is receptive and supportive of the innovation that is being planned than in the details of planning the innovation itself.

Whereas these "tactics" can be discussed and analyzed theoretically in some formal course context, it is once more something that is best learned through the opportunity of application in a context where analytical and evaluative reflection is encouraged and where it may be possible for the dangers of failure of the project to be controlled (e.g., by simulation). Ultimately, however, the trainee must be able to transfer with success the skills of managing the project to the realities of real contexts surrounding real educational problems. So, we are faced with the necessity of placing the training and development of an educational technologist very much within the context of an educational or training institution where real projects are taking place and real forces and pressures are acting within a broader context.

In summary, all of the factors discussed above tend to point to a common set of desirable characteristics in the structure of a training and education program for educational technologists. These characteristics are:

- a real-life work or simulated work-based training context rather than an "ivory tower" context in an institution divorced from the realities of educational innovation;

- more emphasis on problem analysis and solution (whether in real-life, on-job situations, through case studies, or through simulated situations) and support of these activities through self-study materials;
- great variety of problem situations (varying in terms of difficulty, in terms of disciplinary content and in terms of complexity), accessible to the learner through a process of guided negotiation so that appropriate problems are selected for analysis which are neither irrelevant in terms of content or too advanced or difficult in terms of current skill levels but which are always within the interest and desire of the individual learner;
- emphasis on a learning process which involves opportunities to reflect on decisions, and to compare and contrast different approaches to problems, through interaction with both teachers and peers;
- evaluation and the measurement of the level of success in dealing with these problems satisfactorily; and
- emphasis on carrying through the solution to the implementation stage and facing up to surprises caused by the reactions from other systems that make up the overall environment or context of the problem.

## Conclusion

What we have attempted to show is that the education and training problems of the twenty-first century are exceedingly complex and unlikely to be solved by the present forms of higher education and more specifically the current approaches to training educational technologists. We have advocated a broad and holistic understanding and application of the systems approach rather than the narrow and over-simplified algorithms that characterize present interpretations. We need to "regain paradigms lost" in the quest for efficiency and simplicity and maintain a "polyfocal vision" of educational technology. This critical and broader analysis suggests that we are not pitting traditional education against distance education or the conventional classroom against the virtual classroom but rather we are seeking an opening-out of the curriculum, which demands the development of open learning modes that will redefine the classroom of the twenty-first century.

## References

Ackoff, R. L. (1960). Systems, organizations, and interdisciplinary research. *General Systems Yearbook, Vol. 5,* 1–8. Society for General Systems Research.

Barnett, R. (1990). *The Idea of Higher Education.* London: SRHE & Open University Press.

Bates, A. W. (1990). *Third Generation Distance Education: The Challenge of New Technology*. Unpublished Paper. The Open Learning Agency, Vancouver, BC. (ERIC Document Reproduction Service No. ED 332 682).

Beer, S. (1959). *Cybernetics and Management*. London: Methuen.

Boot, R. L. & Hodgson, V. E. (1987). Open learning: Meaning and experience. In V. E. Hodgson (Ed.), *Beyond Distance Teaching: Towards Open Learning*. London: Open University Press.

Carnevale, A. P. (1991, September). Training in the new economy. *Executive Excellence, 8 (9)*, 13.

Carnevale, A. P. & Schulz, E. R. (1990, July). Economic accountability for training: Demands and responses. *Training and Development Journal, 44 (7)*, S.2–S.4.

Criticos, C. (1992). *A Proposal for an Open Learning Master's Degree in Educational Technology*. Unpublished Thesis. Syracuse University, Syracuse, New York.

Daniel, J. (1988). The worlds of open learning. In N. Paine (Ed.), *Open Learning in Transition*. London: Kogan Page.

Drea, J. T. & Armistead, L. D. (1988). *Serving Distant Learners Through Instructional Technologies*. Quincy, IL: John Wood Community College. (ERIC Document Reproduction Service No. ED 289 575).

Elson, J. (1992, April 13). Campus of the future. *Time*, 54–58.

Emery, F. E. (Ed.) (1969). *Systems Thinking*. Harmonsworth, UK: Penguin Books.

Hart, P. (1992, February). *Distance Education at CSUF*. Paper presented at the AECT Conference, Washington DC.

Hawkridge, D. (1991). Challenging educational technology. *Educational and Training Technology International, 28 (2)*, 102–110.

Hlynka, D. & Nelson, B. (1991). Educational technology as metaphor. In D. Hlynka & J. Belland (Eds.), *Paradigms Regained*. Englewood Cliffs, NJ: Educational Technology Publications.

Johnson J. K. (1992). Advancing by degrees: Trends in Master's and Doctoral programs in educational communications and technology. *Tech Trends, 37 (2)*, 13–16.

Knapper, C. (1988). Lifelong learning and distance education. *The American Journal of Distance Education, 2 (1)*, 63–72.

Komoski, P. K. (1987). *Educational Technology: The Closing In or Opening Out of Curriculum and Instruction.* (ERIC Document Reproduction Service No. ED 295 676).

Neil, M. W. (1969). A systems approach to course planning at the Open University. In A. J. Romiszowski (Ed.), *A Systems Approach to Education and Training.* London: Kogan Page.

Neil, M. W. (1970). An operational and systems approach to research strategy in educational technology. In A. P. Mann and C. K. Brunstrom (Eds.), *Aspects of Educational Technology, Vol. III.* London: Pitman.

Palmer, P. J. (1990). Community, conflict and ways of knowing: Ways to deepen our educational agenda. In J. Kendall (Ed.), *Combining Service & Learning, Volume I.* Raleigh, NC: NSIEE.

Pask, G. (1961). *An Approach to Cybernetics.* London: Hutchinson.

Race, P. (1989). *The Open Learning Handbook: Selecting, Designing, and Supporting Open Learning Materials.* London: Kogan Page.

Romiszowski, A. J. (1970). Systems approaches to education and training: An introduction. In A. J. Romiszowski (Ed.), *A Systems Approach to Education and Training.* London: Kogan Page.

Romiszowski, A. J. (1981). *Designing Instructional Systems: Decision-Making in Course Planning and Curriculum Design.* London: Kogan Page.

Romiszowski, A. J. (1991). Applications of educational technology: The international perspective. In G. J. Anglin (Ed.), *Instructional Technology: Past, Present, and Future.* Englewood, CO: Libraries Unlimited.

Schon, D. (1987). *Educating the Reflective Practitioner.* San Francisco: Jossey-Bass.

Smolowe, J. (1992, April 13). The pursuit of excellence. *Time,* 59–60.

Snell, R. S., Hodgson, V. E. & Mann, S. J. (1987). Beyond distance teaching: Towards open learning. In V. E. Hodgson (Ed.) *Beyond Distance Teaching: Towards Open Learning.* London: Open University Press.

Stonier, T. (1988). Education: Society's number-one enterprise. In N. Paine (Ed.), *Open Learning in Transition.* London: Kogan Page.

Stufflebeam, D. L. *et al.* (1971). *Educational Evaluation and Decision-Making.* Itasca, IL: Peacock Publishers.

Wolcott, L. L. (1991, February). *Qualitative Study of Teachers' Planning of Instruction for Adult Learners in a Telecommunications-Based Distance Education Environment.* Paper presented at the AECT Annual Conference, Washington DC. (ERIC Document Reproduction Service No. ED 335 023).

## About the Authors

*Alexander J. Romiszowski* is a Professor in the Instructional Design, Development, and Evaluation program in the School of Education at Syracuse University. Dr. Romiszowski has published many books and articles about educational technology. He has been involved in educational technology projects around the world, including the United Kingdom, India, Hungary, and South America.

*Costas Criticos* is a lecturer in educational technology and director of the media center at the University of Natal in Durban, South Africa. He has been involved in numerous educational technology projects in South Africa. He attended Syracuse University as a Fulbright Scholar, where he received his Master's degree in Instructional Design, Development, and Evaluation.

# 12/ Closing Education's Technology Gap[1]

## Lewis J. Perelman

**Discovery Institute**

*Viewed as an economic sector, education has the worst productivity record of any major U.S. industry. Part of the reason is that education invests a hundred to a thousand times less in research and development than other, information-based businesses. To close the gap, U.S. education and training institutions should set aside at least 1% of their budgets for an R&D fund to be managed by a new National Institute for Learning Technology.*

Education costs too much. At the same time that the learning enterprise—the vast business of education, training, and learning activities—is becoming more crucial to an information age society,[2] the spiralling cost of conventional education's dubious output is becoming a millstone around the neck of the entire national economy. Education's productivity crisis lies at the heart of our country's overall human capital predicament.

---

[1]This chapter originally appeared as Hudson Institute Briefing paper 111. Permission was granted by the Hudson Institute and the author to include it here.

[2]The importance of education and training to the modern economy is by now widely appreciated. For details see William Johnston and Arnold Packer, *Workforce 2000: Work and Workers for the 21st Century* (Indianapolis: Hudson Institute, 1987) and Lewis J. Perelman, *The Learning Enterprise: Adult Learning, Human Capital, and Economic Development* (Washington, DC: Council of State Planning Agencies, 1984).

Emerging initiatives to not merely reform but to "restructure" the nation's educational enterprise in radical ways[3] will be essential to undoing education's productivity malaise. These structural changes—opening public schools to choice and competition, cutting centralized bureaucracy and red tape, holding education and training accountable for actual knowledge and skill gained by students, and revising employment practices to reward competence and flexibility—will finally create an environment where instructional efficiency matters.

But the combination of modern technological and organizational innovations that has enabled productivity to soar in other industries will not occur even in a restructured educational system unless education makes an investment in research and development comparable to other economic sectors. The shocking truth is that, compared to any other major industry, American education's investment in research and innovation is almost nonexistent.

Advocates of restructuring education have tended to overlook the magnitude and importance of education's R&D gap. Closing that gap must be made a top priority item on the restructuring agenda.

## Education's Productivity Crisis

A four-year study by the U.S. Congress' Office of Technology Assessment[4] concluded that the key obstacle thwarting America's shift to an information age economy is the egregiously poor productivity of the education sector. In particular, OTA found that education is tied (with social work) as the most labor-intensive business in the economy, with labor costs equal to 93% of output value, compared to 54% for all private business.

Education's productivity is not only poor but declining. Since 1950, the real dollar (inflation-adjusted) cost of elementary/secondary (K–12) education in the United States has quadrupled! College is no better bargain: The price tag for higher education doubled in the last decade as costs grew much faster than inflation.

Costs zooming upward, enrollments staying the same or declining, and the quality of the output of schools and colleges either staying as good (according to their fans) or deteriorating (according to their critics) altogether mean that educational productivity—in terms of the ratio of effectiveness to cost—has been going sharply downhill.

---

[3]For example, see David Kearns and Denis Doyle, *Winning the Brain Race: A Bold Plan to Make Our Schools Competitive* (San Francisco: ICS Press, 1988).

[4]Henry Kelly, *Technology and the American Economic Transition: Choices for the Future* (Washington, DC: Office of Technology Assessment, 1988).

The immediate cause of this dreary performance is education's gross lack of investment in technology. OTA's study revealed that education has by far the lowest level of capital investment (another name for "buying technology") of any major industry: only about $1,000 per employee. The average for the U.S. economy as a whole is about $50,000 of capital investment per job. Some high-tech industries invest $300,000 or more in technology for each worker. Even other, relatively labor-intensive, "service" businesses provide at least $7,000 to $20,000 worth of equipment and facilities for each employee.

This is a good place to call attention to a unique characteristic of the education industry, or learning enterprise, that sets it apart from all other businesses, and that makes the above and other unflattering companions even worse. That is: Education is the only business where the consumer does the essential work. To the extent that learning is education's essential (though not only) business, it's clear that the productivity of the student or learner—not teachers or administrators—is what ultimately counts.

If we count the student, rather than the paid staff, as the "worker" to be compared to workers in other sectors, education's productivity/technology gap looms even larger. Thus, the public schools' niggling capital investment of $1,000 per employee becomes a pathetic $100 per worker if worker means student. As a matter of fact, while the average U. S. public school budget now comes to about $5,000 per student annually, the typical school district expends only about $100 to $200 of that exorbitant sum on materials and tools for each student to use directly for learning.

In a world where life cycles of product and production technology now are measured in months rather than decades, scanty capital investment inevitably leads to creaking technological backwardness. So we should be dismayed but unsurprised to observe that—in the midst of a global information revolution— the instructional technology available to most students, most of the time, in most American schools and colleges today ranges from 100 to 1,000 years old. While the power of information technology has been leaping upward by factors of 10 every few years since the 1950s, a report a few years ago by the late Ithiel Pool of MIT[5] found that classroom instruction was the only one of some two dozen communications media studied whose productivity sharply declined during the past two decades.

Had the power of educational technology (not in some laboratory but in common use) grown at the same pace over the last four decades as the power of computer technology, a high school or college diploma—which still take 12 and 4 years respectively, to produce, at an average cost for either of about $60,000— could be produced in less than ten minutes for about five cents!

---

[5]Ithiel de Sola Pool, "Tracking the Flow of Information," *Science*, 12 August 1983.

The point is not so much that we should expect instant education for a nickel tomorrow, but that at least we should expect the education industry to make *some* meaningful technological progress in the same direction—forward—as the rest of the economy. This comparison also emphasizes that the technological gap between the school environment and the "real world" is growing so wide, so fast that the educational experience is at risk of becoming not merely unproductive but utterly irrelevant to normal human existence.

## The R&D Gap

Compared to any other part of the modern economy, the minuscule share of the education industry's vast financial resources invested in research and development is shocking. While the federal government pays less than 9% of the national bill for formal education (school and college), it pays for most of the educational research. Depending on what one counts as "R&D," the federal Education Department spent between $136 million and $388 million on some kind of research in the 1989 fiscal year. Only about a million dollars of this was devoted to development of advanced instructional technology. Most of the research on high-tech teaching and learning is financed by the Defense Department, to the tune of about $200 million annually. The National Science Foundation also allocates about $15 million a year to research on innovative instruction for science and mathematics.

These hundreds of millions of dollars may sound like a lot of money for research until one considers the scale of the nation's learning enterprise. The education and training sector is America's largest information industry and, depending on what is counted, may be simply the country's biggest business. Formal instruction provided by schools, colleges, and corporate and military training departments is about a $400 billion a year industry; OTA estimates it employs around 10% of the U. S. workforce.

When on-the-job training and other less visible but no less economically significant forms of teaching and learning are included, the learning enterprise is over a $500 billion business, and may even equal the $600 billion health care industry (generally viewed as the biggest).

By OTA's accounting, the education sector's investment in R&D comes to only 0.025% of its annual revenues. Even if demonstration projects, program evaluations, and other activities plausibly considered "research" are included, education's R&D spending still is less than 0.1% of revenues.

In contrast, R&D accounts for 2.5% of the entire U. S. gross national product. The average American business firm invests 2% of sales in R&D. But in high-tech, information-based businesses—the kind of business education ought to be but isn't—companies commonly plow 7% to 30% of their sales into R&D. For instance, in *Business Week*'s 1989 "R&D Scoreboard" the five top-rated companies in the computer software and services sector (the fastest growing segment of today's computer industry) spent 26.9%, 17.2%, 17.9%, 16.1%, and 28.6% of their revenues on R&D.

. But *Business Week's* research revealed that it is the amount of R&D investment per employee that is the most powerful predictor of business success. By that standard, the magnitude of the education sector's failure to invest in innovation is magnified because education, being so labor intensive, dilutes its already piddling R&D expenditures over a relatively larger workforce than other businesses.

For the formal education sector (kindergarten through university), R&D spending per employee is less than $50 a year. Now consider what each of those leading companies in the computer software and services business spend annually on R&D per employee: $42,622; $36,207; $33,535; $30,389; and $30,264.[6] The composite figure for all the companies in all the industries rated by *Business Week* is $5,042 of annual R&D investment per employee.[7]

As dismal as $50 a year for education's per-employee R&D investment appears, it's instructive again to recall that the student is the "worker" whose productivity most matters in the education business. So the education sector's annual R&D investment per worker realistically is something less than $5—a thousand times less than the norm for other major industries, and ten thousand times less than the amount spent by the most competitive U. S. firms in high-tech, information businesses.

## The Innovation Gap

Clearly, a bold initiative is urgently needed to close education's disastrous R&D gap. But before getting to specific proposals to solve that problem, it's essential to recognize that merely adding dollars to the educational research budget will not, by itself, lead to more innovation or greater productivity in the nation's schools and colleges

The failure to effectively exploit the instructional power of the computer is just one notable illustration of educational institutions' capacity to resist change. A decade and a half into the "desktop computer" revolution, 40 million personal

---

[6]At the bottom of this group of 33 companies was a firm that invested only $790 per employee in R&D last year. The composite (a weighted average) R&D spending per worker of the surveyed companies in this business was $18,428.

[7]The magazine surveyed companies reporting sales of at least $35 million and R&D expenses at least equal to $1 million or 1% of sales. So small firms or those making little investment in innovation are not included. But most academic enrollment is in school districts and public universities whose budgets would make them big businesses compared to companies on the magazine's list. And the point of this paper is that educational organizations should be among the leaders in innovation. So the "Scoreboard" is a relevant yardstick of education's R&D gap.

computers are in use in the United States. Computers called "computers" are in some 20 million American homes. But nearly 30 million U.S. homes have Nintendo "game" units—computer terminals masquerading as toys.

In contrast, another OTA report[8] found that U. S. schools have spent a total of about $2 billion on instructional computers over a period of ten years—that's only a tenth of what the rest of America spends on personal computers every year. A survey by Henry Jay Becker of Johns Hopkins University determined that there are about two million instructional computers in K–12 schools, only about one for every 20 students on average.[9] Many of the computers counted as "present" in schools are old, obsolete, or simply locked away, unused. While experts have concluded that, ideally, all students should get to use instructional computers for about a third of their time in school, or 10 hours a week, the OTA report estimated that students typically get to use computers in U. S. schools only about one hour a week.

There is little mystery about the broad reasons for the failure of schools and colleges to adopt computers and other technological innovations or about what needs to be done, in general, to remedy these institutions' resistance to progress. The key reasons for the lack of adoption of productive technological innovations in U.S. pre-college education lie in the combination of incentives and disincentives common to government-owned, bureaucratically administered, monopolistic enterprises.

In essence, the public school is America's Collective farm. Innovation and productivity are lacking in American education for basically the same reasons they are scarce in Soviet agriculture: absence of competitive, market forces.

The public school normally provides, at best, no incentive—other than altruism or curiosity—for practitioners to adopt innovations. A teacher I interviewed for a recent study of the use of computers in public schools put it succinctly: "Why should I do anything different next year from what I did last year?" In fact, scarcely any schools, even those that aspire to be progressive, offer any substantive reward, or even opportunity, for professional staff to adopt productive tools.

At worst, and commonly, the typical school environment is pregnant with disincentives for innovation which, over a period of a half century or more, have proven highly effective in preventing or reversing technological change in education.

For instance, journalists and other education analysts commonly cite lack of teacher training as a barrier to adoption of instructional computers. Yet training,

---

[8]Linda G. Roberts, *Power On! New Tools for Teaching and Learning* (Washington, DC: Office of Technology Assessment, 1988).

[9]The OTA Report (Roberts, 1988) estimated only one computer for every 30 students.

by itself, cannot overcome bureaucratic disincentives. As Bella Rosenberg of the American Federation of Teachers states bluntly, and correctly: "Teacher training is no substitute for restructuring education." Indeed, training may even prove counterproductive.

The Houston Independent School District, for example, used to provide an intensive, 300 hour teacher training course in the effective use of instructional technology.[10] Yet graduates of the program—the most innovative and technically proficient teachers in the district—who practiced what they had learned actually got negative grades on a state-imposed teacher evaluation instrument that values "teaching" according to the ability to stand in front of a blackboard and talk, rather than the ability, or even willingness, to employ modern, student-centered tools. Staff in the district report that many of the best-trained teachers left the system for jobs where their skills are in demand and rewarded.

Despite apparent institutional differences, the barriers and disincentives for innovation in higher education are broadly similar to and equally effective as those that hobble K–12 schools. The list of such obstacles could be extended indefinitely. But the vast majority stem from the bureaucratic structure of the formal education system, not, as some "experts" claim, from inadequate technology or lack of government subsidies.

In contrast to the situation in schools and colleges, demand for computer-based instruction is strong in the unregulated and unsubsidized market for employer-provided education. It is estimated that some 30% of the more than $50 billion employers invest annually in employee training is spent on computer-based instructional systems—that is, over seven times more in one year than public schools have spent on instructional computers in the last ten years! Or, to look at the same data from another angle, employer-provided education invests a 300 times larger share of its total budget in computer-based instruction than public education does.

The failure to consider the total market for instructional computing and other advanced technology beyond schools commonly distorts published reports of educational technology's lack of progress.[11] Contrary to what many reports imply, the problem is not that instructional computers don't work well enough, or that they are not affordable, or that educators won't use them. The truth is that computer based and other high-tech instructional tools are being produced; sold, and used successfully and extensively outside of schools.

---

[10]The program was terminated this year by a new district superintendent.

[11]For example, see "Computers in School: A Loser? Or a Lost Opportunity?" *Business Week*, 17 July 1989, and "Computers Make Slow Progress in Class," *Science*, 26 May 1989.

The key difference is that competition makes corporate and military trainers accountable for costs and results. And the principal reason for the almost total lack of investment in productivity-enhancing technological innovation, and for the record of steadily declining productivity in formal education, is the inherent absence of competitive, market incentives in the bureaucratic structure of the U. S. educational system.

History argues that neither the abundance of current information technology nor further research and invention of even more exotic tools for teaching and learning will, by themselves, have much impact on the near-static pace of innovation in education. Pocket calculators have been ubiquitous for some two decades, yet their common use in pre-college education is still sedulously resisted. Television has been around for half a century yet its educational use remains largely trivial. The telephone is a century-old technology; yet hardly any school teachers in America have their own office telephones or even ready access to one.

An illuminating study by Douglas Ellson[12] unveiled 125 instructional technologies and methods that, according to published research reports, have been proved capable of at least doubling the productivity of teaching. Yet Ellson observed that the use of these productive tools is virtually unknown in U.S. schools and colleges. Over 20 years of research shows that computer-assisted instruction, properly employed, can produce at least 30% more learning in 40% less time at 30% less cost than traditional classroom teaching. The cost to the U. S. economy of education's failure to adopt these kinds of proven, on-the-shelf teaching technology on a large scale may be as much as $100 billion a year.

Continual attempts to inject technological innovation into American schools and colleges through subsidized experimental, pilot, and demonstration projects or top-down bureaucratic mandates have failed as thoroughly as similar initiatives in the Soviet state agricultural system. In contrast, American agriculture has become the most productive in the world because adoption of technological innovation has been motivated by the competitive forces experienced by independent, market-driven enterprises.

The lesson in this is that the massive increase in educational R&D the country desperately needs will not pay off in actual, productive innovation in American schools without a solid dose of perestroika. That is, public schools will remain technologically backward until they are forced to compete to attract customers (students) who control the revenues the schools earn. And colleges will continue to eschew efficient instructional technology until instruction is unshackled from the priority of faculty research, productivity takes precedence over selectivity,

---

[12]Douglas Ellson, "Improving Technology in Teaching," *Phi Delta Kappan*, October 1986.

and institutions are made to compete to generate real learning, not just elite credentials.

On the other hand, the agenda of educational restructuring that has recently evolved from growing disillusion with conventional "reforms" will bear little fruit unless a vastly expanded share of education's resources is committed to the research that is the wellspring of progress and productivity.

## A Solution to the R&D Gap

To start closing the education industry's yawning R&D gap, I propose the following major initiative that we can call the "Hundred-By-One Plan." These are its main provisions:

1. *Get every education and training institution, organization, and program in the United States to set aside at least 1% of its gross revenues for investment in research and development.*

One percent of revenues for R&D is a painfully modest goal—only half the average R&D spending for U.S. businesses, and far less than is typical in high-tech industries—but it's still at least ten times more than what education now spends. With education and training budgets commonly growing by 5–10% a year, it's hard to imagine that any institution could plausibly argue that taking 1% of its budget away from current operations could cause serious damage. Even greater R&D investment would be welcome, of course, but this minimal amount would get the ball rolling.

2. *The goal of this new investment in educational innovation should be to achieve a 100% increase (a doubling) in the productivity of U. S. education and training by a certain date, say, 1996 or 1998.*

This is the meaning of a "Hundred (percent growth in productivity) By One (percent investment in R&D)." The specific goal is subject to discussion; as noted above, doubling teaching productivity is a rather modest goal that can be achieved with on-the-shelf technology, without any new invention. The important thing is to have a goal clearly defined in terms of the benefits of R&D, not just the amount spent on R&D. This will help remind institutions, policymakers, and taxpayers that dollars allocated to R&D are not a loss to the budget, but will be returned many times over in greater productivity.

3. *These funds will be pooled in a common fund administered by a National Institute for Learning Technology. Contributors will be members of the Institute.*

The main reasons for having a single Institute are administrative efficiency, and to achieve "critical mass" or economies of scale in research projects. But the Institute need not and most likely will not be localized in one building or campus. Rather, most of its research operations would be highly decentralized.

The National Institute might well be formed most expeditiously as a network or consortium of individual state institutes. The specific form of organization and management will be determined by the Institute's members and directors.

An important reason for having the institutions put up the R&D money through the 1% set-aside—rather than rely on subsidies or contributions from others—is that it will increase their motivation to actually adopt innovations. Institutions that have invested their own money in research are likely to be more interested in actually using what they've paid for. One reason that educational institutions have rarely adopted productive innovations demonstrated by research paid for by outsiders is that the institutions have nothing at stake.

By the way, this proposal is not saying that all educational R&D would or should be controlled by the National Institute. If individual states, or school districts, or institutions choose to invest another 5% or 10% or 20% of their budgets in R&D locally or through other consortia, so much the better. The Institute is proposed to assure that—at the least—there is a solid core and critical mass of R&D to serve the nation's learning enterprise.

4. *All "professional" staff of the contributing institutions will automatically become voting Associates of the Institute. Associates will elect the Directors, who will determine the priorities for investing the Institute's funds in research and innovation.*

Equal in importance to the financial ownership of innovation is the psychological "ownership" that comes with participating actively in the processes of discovery and invention. Thus, the "Associate" membership of education/training professionals in the Institute is a crucial part of the Plan. As we know from both the theory and practice of "sociotechnical systems design" (STS) in factory and office automation, the most productive technological innovations are those developed through the active engagement of both customers and front-line production workers—the primary consumers and producers.

5. *Contributing member institutions might be given some preference in the awarding of Institute grants and contracts, to enhance the benefit of membership.*

Receiving research grants should not become an entitlement of membership, or the whole benefit of critical mass in pooling funds would be lost. But, on the other hand, there needs to be some unique advantage of Institute membership to cope with the "freeloader" problem inherent in all R&D programs—that is, that those who do not pay for R&D can get most or all of the benefits of research paid for by others.

One way to deal with freeloaders is to limit communication of research results to members, rather than publishing them openly. But such inhibitions generally undermine the R&D process by reducing critical feedback and curtailing potential applications.

Another possible solution to the freeloader problem, of course, would be for government to compel eligible institutions, by statute or regulation, to set aside a share of their budgets to the R&D fund. But such an arrangement would risk aborting many of the benefits of voluntary association: flexibility, quick response, and freedom from political manipulation and bureaucratic red tape. Public and private educational institutions at least ought to have the opportunity to support a national R&D initiative voluntarily before mandates are considered. The experience of institutions such as the Electric Power Research Institute or the part of the old Bell Laboratories that now is known as Bellcore[13] shows that voluntary, collaborative R&D organizations can be viable and productive.

6. *Since K–12 staff would tend to outnumber higher education and training professionals among Institute Associates,*[14] *some provision might be needed to assure a balance of investment among educational needs.*

For instance, childhood education could be limited to no more than 50% of the total Institute budget. Some such limitation is desirable not only to attract non-school organizations and professionals but also because the nation's education budget and policies currently are unconscionably neglectful of adult, lifelong, and non-school learning needs. The 40 million or so American adults who need basic education generally get only about one dollar of investment for every thousand dollars spent on children's education.

What kinds of research and development would the Institute carry out? The specific agenda would be defined by the board and members, but many of the key topics are easy to discern now. Basic research on how brains and artificial systems think and learn, and the application of such research to the development of teaching and learning systems clearly are high priority subjects. Group learning processes and the interaction between human and nonhuman learning systems need more study.

Measurement is an unglamorous but absolutely essential field that needs far more R&D investment if the learning enterprise is to become as innovative and productive as other information industries. Indeed, at present we have only the vaguest idea what "productivity" in education and training means, much less what it is in particular settings. While the groundswell of public support for

---

[13]Since the breakup of the telephone monopoly, Bellcore (Bell Communications Research) has been jointly supported by the Regional Bell Operating Companies. Bell Labs is now exclusively the R&D center for the AT&T corporation.

[14]Roughly four times as many people are employed in elementary and secondary education as in higher education.

refocusing educational management on achieving concrete, practical outcomes is welcome, in truth we know painfully little about what specific learning outcomes are socially and economically useful, or how best to measure them. We even need better means to assess costs, as well as results, if "accountability" is going to be more than a hollow slogan.

We also need much better information about the scope and performance of the huge sector of our economy I call "the learning enterprise" to manage it effectively. Our current statistics about the formal education system of schools and colleges are remarkably shaky, simplistic, and misleading. And data about the even larger but less formal parts of the learning enterprise—not only corporate and government training programs, but such diffuse yet prodigious media as on-the-job learning, conferences, advertising, reading, television, counseling, sports, religion, voluntary associations, and "simple" conversation— are either scant or nonexistent. Such research as we have indicates that at least 90% and probably more than 98% of human learning takes place outside classrooms and other formal "instructional" settings. A key reason the learning enterprise is such an inefficient market is that both producers and consumers are so badly informed about how it operates and what it offers.

Another critical category for the Institute's research would be on the problems of implementation and diffusion of advanced learning technologies. As noted above, the extreme technological backwardness of American education stems less from a lack of fruitful technology than from a stifling web of institutional barriers to the widespread adoption and use of the valuable technology that already exists. We urgently need a much more subtle and thorough understanding of these barriers and how to eliminate them. We also need to learn a great deal about the kinds of organizational arrangements and incentives that can best accelerate the flexible adoption of learning technology.

In particular, any R&D plan must recognize that commercialization is a legitimate and in fact essential goal of the innovation process. No new technologies will be available to educators or students unless the tools can be sold for more than what they cost to produce. Grants, gifts, subsidies, and deep discounts will not lead to a technological revolution in education but only to another in a long series of dead ends. The Institute's entire program must aim at getting products to be marketed both competitively and profitably.

The proposed Institute would represent the concerns of the deliverers and practitioners of educational services. Broadly, the Institute would focus on supporting basic research (on one end of the innovation spectrum) and on removing institutional barriers to technological change (on the other end). This work should include commercialization of technology as one of its ultimate objectives.

However, even though some members of the Institute will and should be for-profit organizations, the R&D mission of the Institute explicitly should not include the development of particular commercial products. The simple reason is that everything we know about the history of the innovation process indicates that private, entrepreneurial organizations are the most prolific engines of successful product creation and diffusion.

If independent entrepreneurs are deemed too slow to introduce advanced learning products, an initiative parallel to the Institute might be considered to mobilize the producers and vendors of commercial educational products and services. This could be an "Educational Sematech"—a consortium linking vendors in a joint R&D venture. The consortium, like Sematech (a collaboration of major U. S. semiconductor manufacturers), would pool R&D funds and staff contributed by member companies; it also could have a cooperative operating relationship with the Institute that might prove useful to accelerate the commercial application of the Institute's research. As a complement to the Institute's mission, the consortium would focus (in the center of the innovation process) on the development of marketable products.

## From Concept to Action

While creating such a National Institute might at first seem to be a job for the federal government, I would argue that it is unlikely and probably even undesirable that this be a federal initiative.

First, closing the R&D gap between education and the rest of the economy means adding at least $4-8 billion to the current pool of educational R&D funds. While the federal government should contribute more than it currently does, it is simply not going to be able to provide anywhere near this kind of money.

The fact is education and training is mostly a state and local government function in the United States. It makes sense for the institutions that are spending the most money in the education sector to provide the largest share of R&D investment. About 80% of the college enrollment and 90% of the K-12 enrollment are in public institutions, chiefly state and local. Not only do state and local governments provide over 90% of the public funding of education in America, they both traditionally and constitutionally exercise most of the responsibility for education policy. Since local governments are constitutionally only creatures of the state, for the purposes of this proposal, the states are where the action needs to be.

The states are also by and large more flexible, adaptive, and innovative than the federal government. In fact, several state government officials with whom I've discussed this proposal already have expressed considerable interest in taking action on it.

One or a few states setting aside at least 1% of their education budgets for a state R&D fund would form a sufficient base to start building a national program. As suggested earlier, a multi-state consortium would be a highly plausible way to organize the National Institute.

This is not to say that there is nothing the federal government can do to help close education's technology gap. Without getting into details here, the way the federal government now spends several hundred million dollars a year on educational research could be reorganized to achieve far more useful results. The President could use his "bully pulpit" to promote the action needed to bring the National Institute for Learning Technology to life. The federal government also could offer to add 10% to members' contributions to the Institute (a donation proportionate to the federal role in education).

Inevitably, the question will be asked: What is this initiative going to cost? The simplest and most accurate answer is: nothing.

The several billion dollar annual budget to be administered by the National Institute is not proposed as an addition to current education budgets but as a reallocation of existing funds to a more productive purpose. Because the explicit goal of the entire program is to greatly increase the productivity of the learning enterprise, the Institute's funding will be repaid many times over by the hundreds of billions of taxpayer and consumer dollars that will be saved as a result of this investment. The real cost associated with education's technology gap is the huge cost of continuing to do nothing to close it.

Another inevitable question is: Will the education community buy this proposal?

That remains to be seen. But professional educators should support it if they consider where the success of this initiative would lead for them: to a learning enterprise with a much greater capital/labor ratio, employing a smaller number of highly skilled, highly productive, highly compensated, and more autonomous professionals employing an array of extremely powerful technical tools to provide better services to more people at lower cost.

In reality, many educators will not and, in fact, should not support this R&D proposal unless it is linked to the rest of the essential agenda for restructuring American education.

The emerging agenda for educational *perestroika* includes: Empower educators to control the resources and operations of their own schools—what's called "school based management." Give families and students the freedom to choose among public schools. Link funding to enrollment so that schools have to compete for revenues by attracting consumers.

For this kind of market-based system to work, we need realistic accounting for the results we want education to achieve, and meaningful incentives for their attainment. This means, first, replacing current tests with valid measures of the knowledge and skills students really need for either employment or higher education.

The important incentives for students, as Albert Shanker of the American Federation of Teachers has argued, should be that acceptance in a job or a college would depend on the documented achievement of the competencies required for entry to either. For school staff, in addition to the incentives inherent in a market system, Shanker proposes to goad their commitment to restructuring by arranging to award a sizable bonus—perhaps $15,000 to $30,000 per person—every five years or so to the individual schools (in restructured districts) that achieve the greatest improvement in measured outcomes.

While the latter restructuring measures focus on public schools, the same basic agenda applies to higher education and training programs: entrepreneurial management, choice, competition, competency-based instruction and employment, and rewards for performance. Adding the kind of R&D initiative proposed here to close the technology gap makes this a complete prescription for replacing an archaic education system with a 21st-century learning enterprise.

## About the Author

*Lewis J. Perelman* has been a public school teacher, senior scientist at the Jet Propulsion Laboratory, and a planning director for a Fortune 100 corporation. This chapter was written while he directed Project Learning 2001 at the Hudson Institute. He is now a Senior Fellow of the Discovery Institute. The ideas outlined in this chapter are elaborated in his book, *Schools Out: Hyperlearning, New Technology, and the End of Education*, published by William Morrow & Co.

# Index